VIRGINIA TEST PREP

Reading Skills Workbook

Focus on Fiction

Grade 4

ISBN 978-1689894920

TEST MASTER PRESS

www.testmasterpress.com

CONTENTS

Introduction   **4**

Reading Skills Practice Sets   **5**

Practice Set 1: Personal Narrative   5
Practice Set 2: Myth   14
Practice Set 3: Play   24
Practice Set 4: Historical Fiction   34
Practice Set 5: Fables   43
Practice Set 6: Science Fiction   54
Practice Set 7: Poetry   65
Practice Set 8: Nature Myths   76
Practice Set 9: Adventure Story   87
Practice Set 10: Mystery Story   96
Practice Set 11: Legend   106
Practice Set 12: Personal Narrative   117
Practice Set 13: Play   126
Practice Set 14: Poetry   136
Practice Set 15: Fairy Tale   147
Practice Set 16: Historical Fiction   158

Answer Key   **167**

INTRODUCTION
For Parents, Teachers, and Tutors

Virginia's English Language Arts Standards

Student learning and assessment in Virginia is based on the skills listed in the *Standards of Learning* and the *Curriculum Framework*. The reading standards describe how students will be able to read and comprehend fictional texts, literary nonfiction, and poetry. This workbook focuses specifically on giving students experience with a wide range of fictional texts. It provides practice understanding, analyzing, and responding to texts and will develop all the skills that students need.

Understanding and Analyzing Fictional Texts

The state standards and the state tests both focus on using a broad range of challenging fictional texts. This workbook provides practice with a wide variety of passage types. It includes common passage types like myths, fables, personal narratives, and poetry. It also includes more unique types like plays, legends, and historical fiction.

For all the passage types, students are expected to demonstrate in-depth understanding. Students need to use close reading to analyze texts carefully and to look at texts critically. Students need to understand what a text says, as well as recognize craft and structure. Students also need to evaluate texts, respond to texts, and make connections between texts. At the same time, there is a strong focus on using evidence to support answers. This workbook focuses on developing the advanced skills that students are expected to have, while giving students experience with a wide variety of passage types.

Types of Reading Comprehension Questions

The state tests require students to read fictional passages and answer questions to show understanding of the text. The tests include a wide variety of questions, including technology-enhanced questions that use online features. Students will answer multiple choice questions, multiple-select questions where more than one answer is selected, text selection questions where words or sentences are highlighted, written answer questions, and graphic response questions where students complete a table, diagram, or web. This workbook provides practice with a wide range of question types, and each passage also ends with an essay question.

Preparing for the SOL Reading Assessments

Students will be assessed each year by taking the SOL Reading assessments. This workbook will help students master these assessments. It will ensure that students have the ability to analyze and respond to all types of fictional texts, while having the strong skills needed to excel on the test.

Practice Set 1

Personal Narrative

The Big Trip

Instructions

This set has one passage for you to read. The passage is followed by questions.

Read each question carefully. For each multiple choice question, fill in the circle for the correct answer. For other types of questions, follow the instructions given. Some of the questions require a written answer. Write your answer on the lines provided.

The Big Trip
By Elena Porter

It was the last day of school when my mom told me the news. I had just gotten off the bus and ran through the front door when I saw my travel backpack sitting in the hallway. My mom had a big smile on her face and she said, "Pack your bag because we're going on a big trip." I soon found out that my mom, my dad, my little sister and I were going to spend the summer traveling around Asia. Little did I know, this would be the trip of a lifetime!

We headed to the airport to board our first flight to Taiwan. Taiwan is a small island off the coast of China that is about the same size as Louisiana. It may be small, but there was a lot to discover.

We started by exploring the many street markets of Taiwan's capital city, Taipei. These popular walking streets are lined with stalls and stands selling food, drinks, shoes, phones, and so much more! We sampled a lot of dishes such as fried mushrooms, dumplings filled with shrimp, spicy chicken wings, Taiwanese hamburgers, and even an ice cream burrito.

My favorite treat in Taiwan, however, was the bubble tea. Bubble tea is milk tea with chewy little bubbles that you suck through a thick straw. They are so much fun to drink! I loved them so much that I had two bubble teas in one day! We took a break from eating and shopping to visit Taiwan's natural hot springs, which are hot pools of water in the ground. It was so relaxing! We only stayed in Taiwan for one week, but I would have liked to stay longer so that I could have explored more.

After Taiwan, we flew to South Korea. We stayed in the capital city called Seoul where everyone seems to be in a hurry. The city's cars, buses, and taxis never seemed to slow down. The cars whizzed from place to place, and so did the people. The people bustled about and always seemed in a hurry. I even had people knock into me a few times.

The first thing we did in Seoul was go shopping in a big outdoor shopping area. It was very crowded so I had to hold my mom's hand the whole time. My mom bought perfume, my dad bought green tea, and my sister and I bought traditional Korean dresses made of silk. For dinner, we went to a Korean BBQ restaurant where we cooked our own meat! There were lots of side dishes like pickled vegetables, corn salad, and even tiny snails! Afterwards, my clothes smelled like smoke. The rest of the week was spent exploring the city using the underground subway system and visiting many more shopping areas. I loved the way the city lit up at night.

The next country we visited was Thailand. From the moment we stepped out of the airport, the weather was so hot! Luckily, we went straight to the beach in a small town called Krabi. After the rush and crowds of Taipei and Seoul, it was great to be somewhere peaceful.

We spent a lot of time enjoying the wonderful beaches. The ocean water was so clear that I could see my toes! We went snorkeling with tiny colorful fish, a couple of harmless eels, and many gorgeous coral reefs. I had to wear lots of sunscreen so that I didn't burn my skin. My sister and I met two other kids from Germany who invited us to play volleyball on the beach and build sandcastles near the water.

I really loved the food in Thailand, but it was a little bit spicy. I ate spicy rice noodles and drank lots of green coconuts filled with tasty coconut water. After a few days at the beach, we flew to the north of Thailand. There, we visited an elephant sanctuary where we got to feed elephants their favorite snacks such as sugar cane and watermelon. We even got to give the elephants a bath in the muddy river! This was my favorite country on the trip.

For our last stop, we went to India! From the airport, we hopped on an old bus that was headed to the city. However, the bus stopped early because there was a celebration in the street. It was a wedding! All the passengers got off the bus and were invited to dance in the street and eat some local food. Everyone was smiling and seemed so happy. The women were dressed in beautiful skirts that sparkled in the sun. I learned that these outfits are called saris. I also learned that Indian weddings can last for up to 4 days! Sadly, we didn't stay at the wedding for that long.

We got back on the bus, drove to Delhi, and checked into our hotel. During the next few days, we visited the Taj Mahal where we took lots of pictures, ate lots of Indian food such as chicken curry and naan bread, went shopping in traditional outdoor markets, and enjoyed watching the fast-paced traffic in the streets. Before it was time to go home, my sister and I got beautiful henna designs painted on our hands.

The flight home was really long! It took us 19 hours to fly from Delhi to Seattle, but it was fun because I was with my family. We spent most of the time talking about our vacation, looking at silly pictures of my dad eating food from around the region, and admiring the beautiful henna on our hands. The rest of the time was spent watching movies on the plane and sleeping. I will always be grateful to my mom and dad for taking my sister and I on such a life-changing trip. My summer trip around Asia has inspired me to learn more about different cultures and to travel the world on my own one day.

1   What can you tell from the first paragraph of the passage?

    Ⓐ   The trip is a surprise to Elena.

    Ⓑ   The trip is a special present for Elena.

    Ⓒ   Elena had been asking to visit Asia for a long time.

    Ⓓ   Elena had never visited another country before.

2   In paragraph 3, the author describes how they "sampled a lot of dishes." What does the word *sampled* mainly show?

    Ⓐ   They all shared the food.

    Ⓑ   They paid a lot for the food.

    Ⓒ   They ate the food with their hands.

    Ⓓ   They tried a little bit of each dish.

3   What idea about Taiwan is best supported by the map?

    Ⓐ   Taiwan is an island.

    Ⓑ   Taiwan is near China.

    Ⓒ   Taiwan is a busy place.

    Ⓓ   Taiwan is about the size of Louisiana.

4   Which sentence from paragraph 4 gives a definition?

    Ⓐ   *My favorite treat in Taiwan, however, was the bubble tea.*

    Ⓑ   *Bubble tea is milk tea with chewy little bubbles that you suck through a thick straw.*

    Ⓒ   *They are so much fun to drink!*

    Ⓓ   *I loved them so much that I had two bubble teas in one day!*

5   Which word best describes Seoul?

    Ⓐ   busy

    Ⓑ   noisy

    Ⓒ   relaxing

    Ⓓ   scenic

6   List **two** details that support your answer to Question 5.

1: _____

_____

2: _____

_____

7   Complete the table below by listing what each family member bought in Seoul.

Person	Item Bought
Elena's mother	
Elena's father	
Elena's sister	

8   Complete the web below by listing **three** activities Elena did on the beaches of Krabi.

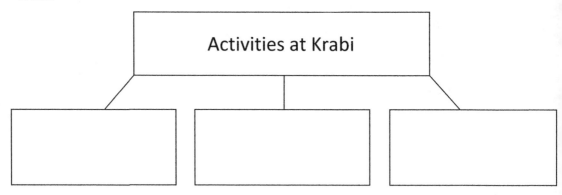

Activities at Krabi

9   Select the **two** items that Elena ate or drank in Thailand.

☐   corn salad   ☐   spicy chicken wings

☐   green coconuts   ☐   ice cream burrito

☐   sugar cane   ☐   pickled vegetables

☐   naan bread   ☐   spicy rice noodles

☐   bubble tea   ☐   shrimp dumplings

10 The mood of the wedding in India is best described as –

Ⓐ wild and crazy

Ⓑ happy and joyful

Ⓒ calm and peaceful

Ⓓ sweet and loving

11 Complete each sentence by listing **one** thing that was similar about Delhi and Taipei and **one** thing that was similar about Delhi and Seoul.

Delhi and Taipei both _____

_____

Delhi and Seoul both _____

_____

12 Which sentence from the last paragraph best supports the idea that Elena appreciates her parents taking her to Asia?

Ⓐ *It took us 19 hours to fly from Delhi to Seattle, but it was fun because I was with my family.*

Ⓑ *We spent most of the time talking about our vacation, looking at silly pictures of my dad eating food from around the region, and admiring the beautiful henna on our hands.*

Ⓒ *I will always be grateful to my mom and dad for taking my sister and I on such a life-changing trip.*

Ⓓ *My summer trip around Asia has inspired me to learn more about different cultures and to travel the world on my own one day.*

13 Select the **one** thing that Elena and her family do in every Asian country they visit.

☐   shop at markets

☐   use the subway

☐   buy souvenirs

☐   try the local foods

☐   meet new people

☐   visit famous landmarks

14 Read this sentence from the first paragraph.

Little did I know, this would be the trip of a lifetime!

What does the phrase "trip of a lifetime" show about the trip? Explain your answer.

_____

_____

_____

_____

_____

15   How is Elena's time in Thailand different from her time in Taiwan, South Korea, and India? Use **three** details from the passage in your answer.

_____

_____

_____

_____

_____

_____

_____

_____

_____

_____

_____

_____

_____

Practice Set 2

Myth

The Stonecutter

Instructions

This set has one passage for you to read. The passage is followed by questions.

Read each question carefully. For each multiple choice question, fill in the circle for the correct answer. For other types of questions, follow the instructions given. Some of the questions require a written answer. Write your answer on the lines provided.

The Stonecutter
Adapted from a Japanese Folktale

Once upon a time there lived a stonecutter, who went every day to a great rock in the side of a big mountain and cut out slabs for houses. He understood very well the kinds of stones wanted for different purposes, and as he was also a careful workman he had plenty of customers. For a long time he was happy and content, and asked for nothing but what he had.

Now in the mountain dwelt a spirit which now and then appeared to men, and helped them in many ways to become rich and prosperous. The stonecutter, however, had never seen this spirit, and only shook his head, with an unbelieving air, when anyone spoke of it. But a time was coming when he learned to change his opinion.

One day the stonecutter carried a beautiful rock slab to the house of a rich man, and saw there all sorts of beautiful things, of which he had never even dreamed. Suddenly his daily work seemed to grow harder and heavier, and he said to himself: "Oh, if only I were a rich man, and could sleep in a bed with silken curtains and golden tassels, how happy I should be!"

And a voice answered him: "Your wish is heard; a rich man you shall be!"

At the sound of the voice the stonecutter looked round, but could see nobody. He thought it was all his fancy, and picked up his tools and went home early, for he did not feel inclined to do any more work that day. But when he reached the little house where he lived, he stood still with amazement, for instead of his wooden hut was a stately palace filled with splendid furniture. Most splendid of all was the bed, in every respect like the one he had envied. He was nearly beside himself with joy. In his new life, the old one was soon forgotten.

It was now the beginning of summer, and each day the sun blazed more fiercely. One morning it was so scorching that the stonecutter could scarcely breathe, and he determined he would stay at home till the evening. He was rather dull, for he had never learned how to amuse himself, and was peeping through the closed blinds to see what was going on in the street, when a little carriage passed by, drawn by servants dressed in blue and silver. In the carriage sat a prince, and over his head a golden umbrella was held, to protect him from the sun's rays.

"Oh, if I were only a prince!" said the stonecutter to himself, as the carriage vanished round the corner. "Oh, if I were only a prince, and could go in such a carriage and have a golden umbrella held over me, how happy I should be!"

And the voice of the mountain spirit answered: "Your wish is heard; a prince you shall be."

And a prince he was. Before and after his carriage rode a company of men; servants dressed in scarlet and gold bore him along, the coveted umbrella was held over his head, everything the heart could desire was his. But yet it was not enough. He looked around for something to wish for, and when he saw that in spite of the water he poured on his grass the rays of the sun scorched it, and that in spite of the umbrella held over his head each day his face grew browner, he cried in his anger: "The sun is mightier than I. If I were only the sun!"

And the mountain spirit answered: "Your wish is heard; the sun you shall be."

And the sun he was, and felt himself proud in his power. He shot his beams above and below, on earth and in heaven; he burnt up the grass in the fields and scorched the faces of princes as well as of poorer folk. But in a short time he began to grow tired of his might, for there seemed nothing left for him to do. Discontent once more filled his soul, and when a cloud covered his face, and hid the earth from him, he cried in his anger: "Does the cloud hold captive my rays, and is it mightier than I? Oh, that I were a cloud, and mightier than any!"

And the mountain spirit answered: "Your wish is heard; a cloud you shall be!"

And a cloud he was. He caught the sun's beams and held them, and to his joy the earth grew green again and flowers blossomed. But that was not enough for him, and for days and weeks he poured forth rain till the rivers overflowed their banks, and the crops of rice stood in water. Towns and villages were destroyed by the power of the rain. Only the great rock on the mountain side remained unmoved. The cloud was amazed at the sight, and cried in wonder: "Is the rock, then, mightier than I? Oh, if I were only the rock!"

And the mountain spirit answered: "Your wish is heard; the rock you shall be!"

And the rock he was, and gloried in his power. Proudly he stood, and neither the heat of the sun nor the force of the rain could move him. "This is better than all!" he said to himself. But one day he heard a strange noise at his feet, and when he looked down to see what it could be, he saw a stonecutter driving tools into his surface. Even while he looked a trembling feeling ran all through him, and a great block broke off and fell upon the ground. Then he cried in his wrath: "Is a mere child of earth mightier than a rock? Oh, if I were only a man!"

And the mountain spirit answered: "Your wish is heard. A man once more you shall be!"

And a man he was, and in the sweat of his brow he toiled again at his trade of stone-cutting. His bed was hard and his food scanty, but he had learned to be satisfied with it, and did not long to be something or somebody else. And as he never desired to be greater and mightier than other people, he was happy at last, and heard the voice of the mountain spirit no longer.

1   What does the first paragraph show about the stonecutter?

     Ⓐ   He dislikes his work.

     Ⓑ   His work has made him rich.

     Ⓒ   He is happy with his work and his life.

     Ⓓ   He is becoming too old to keep working.

2   Read this sentence from the passage.

He understood very well the kinds of stones wanted for different purposes, and as he was also a careful workman he had plenty of customers.

Which of these best describes how the information in the sentence is organized?

     Ⓐ   cause and effect

     Ⓑ   problem and solution

     Ⓒ   fact and opinion

     Ⓓ   main idea and supporting details

3   The second paragraph describes how the stonecutter shook his head "with an unbelieving air" when anyone spoke of the spirit. What does this phrase show about the stonecutter?

     Ⓐ   He is afraid of the spirit.

     Ⓑ   He has searched for the spirit.

     Ⓒ   He wishes the spirit would help him.

     Ⓓ   He does not think that the spirit is real.

4   Complete the table by listing a detail from each paragraph that supports the idea that the stonecutter is not as interested in his work as before.

Details that Show the Stonecutter is Losing Interest in His Work

Paragraph	Detail
3	
5	

5   Read this sentence from the passage.

> **But when he reached the little house where he lived, he stood still with amazement, for instead of his wooden hut was a stately palace filled with splendid furniture.**

What does the word *stately* mean?

    Ⓐ   ancient

    Ⓑ   grand

    Ⓒ   lively

    Ⓓ   magic

6   Select the **three** words the author uses in paragraph 6 to emphasize the heat of the sun.

☐   beginning   ☐   morning

☐   summer   ☐   scorching

☐   blazed   ☐   breathe

☐   fiercely   ☐   determined

7   Which of these does the stonecutter seem to envy most about the prince he sees?

Ⓐ   the carriage he travels in

Ⓑ   the servants working for him

Ⓒ   the freedom available to him

Ⓓ   the umbrella shading him

8   Complete the web below by listing **three** ways the stonecutter does damage when he is a cloud.

Damage Done by the Cloud

9   The stonecutter mainly changes from one thing to another because he is seeking greater –

Ⓐ   freedom

Ⓑ   joy

Ⓒ   power

Ⓓ   purpose

10   The message of the passage is mostly about –

Ⓐ   using your powers to help others

Ⓑ   taking pride in your work

Ⓒ   appreciating what you have

Ⓓ   ignoring other people's opinions

11   How does visiting the rich man's house change the stonecutter? Use **two** details from the passage to support your answer.

_____

_____

_____

_____

_____

12   Paragraph 9 describes how the stonecutter becomes a prince. List **two** details from the paragraph that show that he is still not satisfied with what he has.

1: _____

_____

2: _____

_____

13   The stonecutter is a realistic character, but the events of the passage are not realistic. Explain how you can tell that the events could not really happen. Use **two** details from the passage to support your answer.

_____

_____

_____

_____

_____

14 Complete the diagram to show the things the stonecutter becomes in order from first to last.

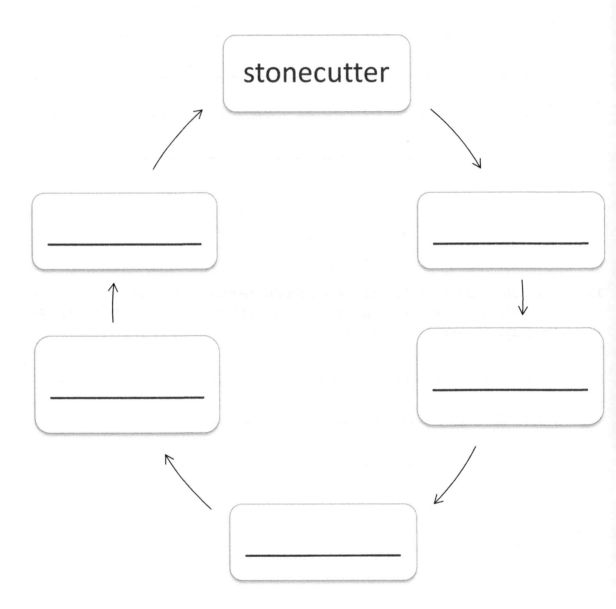

15   How does the stonecutter learn to be satisfied with what he has? Use **three** details from the passage to support your answer.

_____

_____

_____

_____

_____

_____

_____

_____

_____

_____

_____

_____

_____

_____

_____

_____

Practice Set 3

Play

The Bird with the Broken Wing

Instructions

This set has one passage for you to read. The passage is followed by questions.

Read each question carefully. For each multiple choice question, fill in the circle for the correct answer. For other types of questions, follow the instructions given. Some of the questions require a written answer. Write your answer on the lines provided.

The Bird with the Broken Wing

Scene I — *In the Forest, Late Afternoon*

The Oak: See that flock of birds coming! The winter is near and they are flying south.

The Maple: I hope they will not light on my branches; I like to keep my leaves in order.

The Willow: So many birds will break my tender twigs. I am sure I do not want them either. Here they come!

[*The birds fly over the trees.*]

Little Bird: Oh, I can fly no farther! My wing is broken and I cannot hold it up. I am so tired and cold and hungry! I must rest tonight in this forest. I am sure some big strong tree will give me a resting place. I will ask this tall oak, he looks so strong and his leaves are so thick and warm! May I rest in your branches tonight, great oak tree? I am a poor little bird with a broken wing and I am cold and tired and hungry.

The Oak: I am sorry; but my branches are all engaged by the squirrels, who are getting their acorns in for the winter. I have no room for strange birds.

Little Bird: Oh! I am so lonely, so tired! Surely the handsome maple tree will take me in. He has no acorns and so the squirrels will not be in his branches. Kind, lovely maple tree, may I rest tonight in your branches? I am a poor little bird with a broken wing. I will not harm your pretty leaves.

The Maple: My leaves tremble to think of taking in strange birds! My house is in perfect order and I cannot think of disturbing it. Please go away!

Little Bird: Oh, what shall I do? The oak and the maple are so unkind. I am shivering with cold and weak with hunger. Surely *some* tree must be kind. Dear willow tree, you are kind, are you not? Will you take me upon your graceful branches just for tonight?

The Willow: Really, little bird with the broken wing, I think you should have gone on with the other birds. I cannot take you in. I do not know your name or anything about you. Besides, I am very sleepy, and so, goodnight!

Little Bird: Oh, my dear bird friends, how I wish some of you were here! I shall perish with the cold if I must stay on the ground. Where can I go? The oak, the maple, and the willow have all turned me away and the night is coming on.

The Spruce: Dear little bird with the broken wing, come to me! Can you hop up into my branches if I hold them down to you? See, here I am! I am not as handsome as the maple, but my leaves grow thick and I'll try to keep you warm through the night. Come!

Little Bird: Dear spruce tree, how kind you are! I did not see you at first. Yes, here I am, on your lowest branch. How cozy and warm I feel. Oh, you are so good, and I was so tired and cold. Here I'll rest. I wish I could ever thank you enough for your goodness.

The Spruce: Do not speak of that, dear little bird. I am ashamed of the proud, selfish trees that would not shelter you. Should we not all be kind and helpful to one another?

The Pine: Well said, sister spruce. And I will do my best to help you. I am not as strong as the oak, little bird, but I will stand between you and the cold north wind. Rest warm and safe in the branches of the kind spruce tree.

Little Bird: I thank you, tall pine tree, for your kindness. You are a good brother of the spruce and I shall rest well while you are both taking care of me.

The Juniper: I cannot keep the strong north wind from you, little bird with the broken wing, but if you are hungry, you may eat of my berries. Perhaps then you will rest better.

Little Bird: Thank you, dear juniper tree. Why are you all so kind to me? Your berries are good and now I am cold and hungry no longer. I'll go to sleep. Goodnight, dear trees!

Trees: Goodnight, little bird, and may you have sweet dreams!

Scene II — *Midnight in the Forest*

Jack Frost: Here I am in the great forest. How I dislike to touch all these beautiful leaves; yet I must obey the orders of King Winter. Here comes the Forest Fairy. Do you know why I have come, dear Fairy of the Forest?

Forest Fairy: Yes, Mr. Frost. I know that you must touch all the leaves, turning them into brilliant hues of gold and crimson and brown. I dislike to have them go, and yet you and I must obey the commands of King Winter. But,—

Jack Frost: But what, dear Fairy? You speak as if you had some wish to make—what is it?

Forest Fairy: I must tell you. Such a dear little bird came to the forest this evening. He had a broken wing, and he was cold and very tired. He asked shelter from the great oak, the proud maple, and the graceful willow,—and all refused. I was so ashamed of my trees!

Jack Frost: What! Did all the trees refuse to help a poor, tired little bird?

Forest Fairy: Listen! Just as I was in tending to speak to the trees, I heard the spruce tell him to come to her branches and she would give him shelter. Then the pine offered to keep the north wind from him, and the juniper gave him her berries to eat. Could you, dear Jack Frost—

Jack Frost: Yes, yes, I know what you would ask. Such kindness as this should meet with some reward. The leaves of the proud oak, the maple, and the willow shall fall to the ground when the cold of winter comes; but the spruce, the pine, the juniper, and all their family shall keep their leaves and they shall be green all through the year. They shall be called the Evergreen Trees.

1   Draw lines to match the type of tree with the reason the tree does not want birds to rest in its branches.

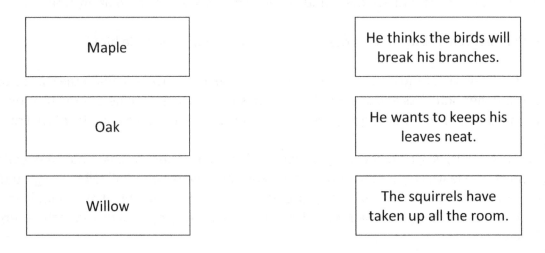

2   Complete the web below by listing **two** more things the little bird complains of being the first time he speaks.

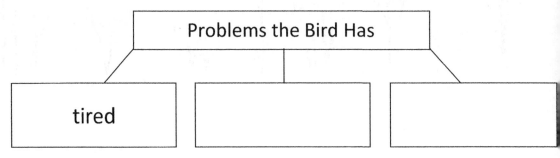

3   What two things does the little bird describe the maple tree as when he asks to rest his branches?

Ⓐ   strong and sturdy

Ⓑ   beautiful and graceful

Ⓒ   kind and lovely

Ⓓ   cozy and warm

4   Select the sentence from the little bird's dialogue that suggests that the bird will be in danger if he cannot find somewhere to rest. Select the **one** best answer.

☐   Oh, what shall I do?

☐   The oak and the maple are so unkind.

☐   I am shivering with cold and weak with hunger.

☐   Surely *some* tree must be kind.

☐   Dear willow tree, you are kind, are you not?

☐   Will you take me upon your graceful branches just for tonight?

5   Describe **two** ways the spruce shows kindness to the little bird.

1: _____

_____

2: _____

_____

6   How does the little bird most likely feel when the spruce offers to take him in?

Ⓐ   doubtful

Ⓑ   grateful

Ⓒ   sleepy

Ⓓ   surprised

7   Complete the table by listing how each tree helps the little bird.

Tree	How it Helps the Little Bird
Spruce	provides a place to rest
Pine	
Juniper	

8   Read the last lines from Scene I.

> **Little Bird: Thank you, dear juniper tree. Why are you all so kind to me? Your berries are good, and now I am cold and hungry no longer. I'll go to sleep. Goodnight, dear trees!**
>
> **Trees: Goodnight, little bird, and may you have sweet dreams!**

These lines mainly emphasize that the little bird is –

Ⓐ   content

Ⓑ   curious

Ⓒ   lonely

Ⓓ   tired

9   Which of these describes the settings of Scene I and Scene II?

Ⓐ   same time, same place

Ⓑ   same time, different place

Ⓒ   different time, same place

Ⓓ   different time, different place

10 Read this sentence spoken by the Forest Fairy.

> **I know that you must touch all the leaves, turning them into brilliant hues of gold and crimson and brown.**

As it is used in the line, what does the word *brilliant* mean?

Ⓐ   bright

Ⓑ   clever

Ⓒ   talented

Ⓓ   unusual

11 How does Jack Frost feel when he first learns that the oak, maple, and willow trees did not help the little bird?

Ⓐ   doubtful

Ⓑ   jealous

Ⓒ   puzzled

Ⓓ   shocked

12 Do you think the oak, maple, and willow trees are selfish? Explain why you feel that way.

_____

_____

_____

_____

_____

13   Read this line from the play.

> **Little Bird: Oh, I can fly no farther! My wing is broken and I cannot hold it up. I am so tired and cold and hungry! I must rest tonight in this forest. I am sure some big strong tree will give me a resting place. I will ask this tall oak, he looks so strong and his leaves are so thick and warm! May I rest in your branches tonight, great oak tree? I am a poor little bird with a broken wing and I am cold and tired and hungry.**

How do these words make the reader feel sorry for the little bird? Use **two** details from the line to support your answer.

_____

_____

_____

_____

14   How are winter and frost personified in the play? Explain your answer.

_____

_____

_____

_____

15   How are the spruce, pine, and juniper trees different from the other trees in Scene I? How does this affect how they are treated by Jack Frost in Scene II? Use **three** details from the play in your answer.

_____

_____

_____

_____

_____

_____

_____

_____

_____

_____

_____

_____

_____

_____

_____

_____

Practice Set 4

Historical Fiction

Life as a Forty-Niner

Instructions

This set has one passage for you to read. The passage is followed by questions.

Read each question carefully. For each multiple choice question, fill in the circle for the correct answer. For other types of questions, follow the instructions given. Some of the questions require a written answer. Write your answer on the lines provided.

Life as a Forty-Niner

The news spread through the world like wild fire. One afternoon, my brother James came running into the kitchen. "They've found gold in California. And plenty of it!" he exclaimed. I looked at my other brother Theodore. I knew what he was thinking. This was our chance to make a break. Our chance for something better. A life of wealth and luxury awaited us!

We boarded a boat headed for San Francisco in 1849. The trip was long and tiring. Not to mention, Theodore spent many nights over the side of the ship with sea sickness. Whenever I would raise my concerns with James, he would always say "high risk for high reward, Henry." I would look up into the night sky and think about his words at length.

From San Francisco, we made the long journey to Coloma on horseback. Once we reached Coloma, we set up camp there for the first night. We laid out all the food and supplies we had. We had everything we needed. The future was bright and our spirits were high.

We built a small cabin using wood from the overhanging trees. It was basically one big room. There was a fireplace in the eastern corner. We fashioned a chimney to take all the smoke from the fire outside. We spent many cold, snowy nights huddled around that fire.

Every day we gathered our tools and panned for gold. James was so positive about our new life as prospectors. In reality, though, life as a forty-niner was far from easy or luxurious. Digging and panning for gold was back-breaking work. We worked long hours and recovered very little gold. We made barely enough to pay for our next meal.

Living conditions were poor. Our cabin always seemed to be damp. We slept on the floor with rats and bugs crawling over us at night. The dampness would often lead to sickness and we were with fever on many occasions.

We tried to work our way through the tough times by getting up earlier and coming home later. Still, we could never seem to find enough gold to make any sort of profit.

On top of all this, there was one gang of thieves who would just come right in and take what you had found. I can remember many times when James, Theodore, and I would try and protect our gold. But 10 or more men would just appear from nowhere. They had weapons and they wanted our spoil. What could we do? We felt scared for our lives. So much gold was given over to these unruly bandits.

We wanted to get out, but we had spent all our funds just making our way to California and getting set up. The gold was drying up day by day. With no money and barely any gold, we were stuck there. We needed a plan. A plan to get us out of there.

James, Theodore, and I had been trying different spots for some time. Although, there was a particular area we hadn't worked. It was a little way back from the river and out of sight. We hadn't worked it because there was no water for panning. If we could take water to that spot we could at least try and see what was there.

We didn't want anyone to find out about what we were doing. So, we decided to go pan our secret spot at night. We worked a normal day in the fields. Then, upon returning home, we had our regular meal of potato and bean soup. We didn't get changed and we didn't wash.

About 8 p.m., we headed out again. James went to the river to fetch two large buckets of water. Theodore and I carried a large copper basin to the new panning spot and waited for James to return. When he returned, he poured the buckets of water into the basin. We took two deep shovels of sand at a time and dumped them in the basin. We began to pan.

Well, you wouldn't believe our luck. We found a decent amount of gold! We had to contain our excitement so as not to stir others in the neighborhood. In fact, by midnight, we had enough gold to buy our ticket out of California.

We realized then that it was time to go. We could not delay. If we stayed in Coloma for any length of time, gangs would surely come and steal our bounty from us.

We went home immediately, and by 1 a.m., by the cover of darkness, we were packing all our things and some supplies for our journey back to San Francisco. By 2 a.m., we had everything on horseback and we set out.

The trip was difficult, but we made San Francisco in good time. We cashed in our gold and bought a ticket for the next ship leaving San Francisco. When we left port that day, we felt so relieved. Sure, we had hoped for a better life. But in the end, we were glad we left with our lives.

1   Read this sentence from the passage.

The news spread through the world like wild fire.

This means that the news –

Ⓐ   traveled slowly

Ⓑ   traveled quickly

Ⓒ   created fear

Ⓓ   created excitement

2   What does the first paragraph suggest about how the brothers feel about finding gold?

Ⓐ   They understand the risks they are taking.

Ⓑ   They think making it rich will be easy.

Ⓒ   They know they will have to work hard.

Ⓓ   They worry that everyone else will be rushing to find it.

3   Based on the first two paragraphs, the brothers mainly see gold as a way to –

Ⓐ   stay together

Ⓑ   become famous

Ⓒ   travel the world

Ⓓ   improve their lives

4 How do the first two paragraphs suggest that the narrator is different from his brothers James and Theodore?

Ⓐ   He is more determined.

Ⓑ   He is more cautious.

Ⓒ   He is more organized.

Ⓓ   He is more patient.

5 How do the brothers travel from San Francisco to Coloma?

Ⓐ   walking

Ⓑ   on trains

Ⓒ   riding horses

Ⓓ   hitching rides

6 Which sentence from paragraph 3 best shows that the brothers felt positive when the first arrived in Coloma?

Ⓐ   *Once we reached Coloma, we set up camp there for the first night.*

Ⓑ   *We laid out all the food and supplies we had.*

Ⓒ   *We had everything we needed.*

Ⓓ   *The future was bright and our spirits were high.*

7   According to the passage, why is the fire in the cabin important?

  Ⓐ It cooks their food.

  Ⓑ It keeps them warm.

  Ⓒ It gives them hope.

  Ⓓ It dries their clothes.

8   In paragraph 6, the author states that "living conditions were poor." List **two** details the author includes to support this statement.

1: _____

_____

2: _____

_____

9   Read this sentence from the passage.

  The gold was drying up day by day.

What does this sentence mean?

  Ⓐ The gold was being stolen.

  Ⓑ The gold was worth less.

  Ⓒ The gold was harder to find.

  Ⓓ The gold was causing arguments.

10 Select the **three** sentences that best show that the brothers could never get ahead no matter how hard they worked.

☐ Every day we gathered our tools and panned for gold.

☐ James was so positive about our new life as prospectors.

☐ In reality, though, life as a forty-niner was far from easy or luxurious.

☐ Digging and panning for gold was back-breaking work.

☐ We worked long hours and recovered very little gold.

☐ We made barely enough to pay for our next meal.

☐ Living conditions were poor.

☐ Our cabin always seemed to be damp.

☐ We slept on the floor with rats and bugs crawling over us at night.

☐ The dampness would often lead to sickness and we were with fever on many occasions.

☐ We tried to work our way through the tough times by getting up earlier and coming home later.

☐ Still, we could never seem to find enough gold to make any sort of profit.

11 Why was the secret spot the brothers mined more difficult than other areas?

Ⓐ It was far from their camp.

Ⓑ They had to carry water to it.

Ⓒ The ground was hard.

Ⓓ It was hidden from the main areas.

12 The narrator describes how gangs of thieves stole gold. Why didn't the brothers fight back? Use **two** details from the passage to support your answer.

_____

_____

_____

_____

_____

13 Why do you think the brothers decided to mine the new spot secretly? Use **two** details from the passage to support your answer.

_____

_____

_____

_____

_____

14 At the end of the passage, the brothers finally find a decent amount of gold. Describe **two** actions that show that they only care about getting home.

1: _____

_____

2: _____

_____

15   The brothers find that the trip to California is not as easy as they imagined. Describe **three** reasons their time in the gold fields is difficult. Use relevant details from the passage to support your answer.

_____

_____

_____

_____

_____

_____

_____

_____

_____

_____

_____

_____

_____

_____

_____

_____

Practice Set 5

Fables

Set of Two Fables

Instructions

This set has two passages for you to read. Each passage is followed by questions.

Read each question carefully. For each multiple choice question, fill in the circle for the correct answer. For other types of questions, follow the instructions given. Some of the questions require a written answer. Write your answer on the lines provided.

The Donkey and the Lap Dog

There was once a donkey whose master also owned a lap dog. This dog was a favorite and received many a pat and kind word from his master, as well as choice bits from his plate. Every day the dog would run to meet the master, frisking playfully about and leaping up to lick his hands and face.

All this the donkey saw with much discontent. Though he was well fed, he had much work to do. Besides, the master hardly ever took any notice of him.

Now the donkey got it into his silly head that all he had to do to win his master's favor was to act like the dog. So one day he left his stable and clattered eagerly into the house.

Finding his master seated at the dinner table, he kicked up his heels and, with a loud bray, pranced giddily around the table, upsetting it as he did so. Then he planted his forefeet on his master's knees and rolled out his tongue to lick the master's face, as he had seen the dog do. But his weight upset the chair, and the donkey and the man rolled over together in the pile of broken dishes from the table.

The master was much alarmed at the strange behavior of the donkey, and calling for help, soon attracted the attention of the servants. When they saw the danger the master was in from the clumsy beast, they set upon the donkey and drove him back to the stable. There they left him to mourn the foolishness that had brought him nothing but a quick march back to where he belonged.

"I have brought it all upon myself," he groaned to himself. "Why couldn't I have been happy with my role in life instead of wanting an idle life like that lazy spoiled dog?" And with those thoughts, he made a decision to please his master by working hard like a good donkey should.

1   Use details from the first paragraph to complete the web with **three** things the
dog receives from his master.

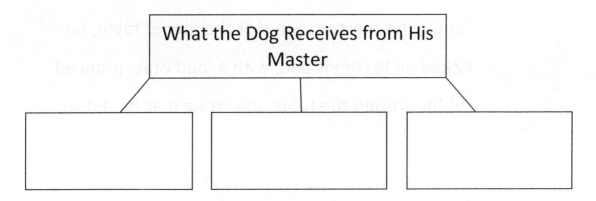

2   According to the first two paragraphs, how does the donkey feel about the lap dog?

Ⓐ   He is angry with him.

Ⓑ   He is jealous of him.

Ⓒ   He is afraid of him.

Ⓓ   He is mistrusting of him.

3   What is the donkey mainly upset about?

Ⓐ   not getting enough food

Ⓑ   not getting enough attention

Ⓒ   having to work too hard

Ⓓ   having to sleep in the stables

4   Circle **two** phrases from the sentence below that suggest that the donkey is enthusiastic.

> ## Finding his master seated at the dinner table, he kicked up his heels and, with a loud bray, pranced giddily around the table, upsetting it as he did so.

5   Which sentence best explains why the donkey decides to act as he does in paragraph 4? Select the **one** best answer.

☐   There was once a donkey whose master also owned a lap dog.

☐   This dog was a favorite and received many a pat and kind word from his master as well as choice bits from his plate.

☐   Every day the dog would run to meet the master, frisking playfully about and leaping up to lick his hands and face.

☐   All this the donkey saw with much discontent.

☐   Though he was well fed, he had much work to do.

☐   Besides, the master hardly ever took any notice of him.

☐   Now the donkey got it into his silly head that all he had to do to win his master favor was to act like the dog.

☐   So one day he left his stable and clattered eagerly into the house.

6   Complete the missing information in the cause and effect diagram below to summarize the donkey's actions and the accident it causes.

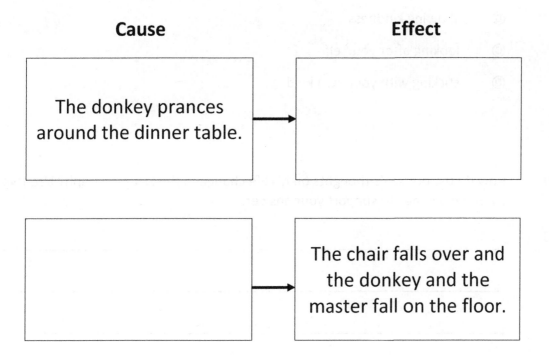

Cause

The donkey prances around the dinner table.

Effect

The chair falls over and the donkey and the master fall on the floor.

7   How does the master feel about the donkey's actions?

Ⓐ   He thinks the situation is funny.

Ⓑ   He is confused and frightened.

Ⓒ   He is angry that the donkey is disobeying him.

Ⓓ   He realizes he has been treating him poorly.

8   The main lesson the reader can learn from the donkey is about –

Ⓐ   being yourself

Ⓑ   showing kindness

Ⓒ   looking after yourself

Ⓓ   sticking with your own kind

9   How do the donkey's thoughts on his life change in the last paragraph? Use **two** detail
from the passage to support your answer.

_____

_____

_____

_____

_____

10   "The Donkey and the Lap Dog" can be described as a humorous story. Describe how
the story is humorous. Use **two** details from the passage to support your answer.

_____

_____

_____

_____

_____

Mercury and the Woodcutter

A poor woodcutter was cutting down a tree near the edge of a deep pool in the forest. It was late in the day and the woodcutter was tired. He had been working since sunrise and his strokes were not so sure as they had been early that morning. Thus it happened that the axe slipped and flew out of his hands into the pool.

The woodcutter was in despair. The axe was all he possessed with which to make a living, and he had not money enough to buy a new one. As he stood wringing his hands and weeping, the god Mercury suddenly appeared and asked what the trouble was. The woodcutter told what had happened, and straightway the kind Mercury dived into the pool. When he came up again he held a wonderful golden axe.

"Is this your axe?" Mercury asked the woodcutter.

"No," answered the honest woodcutter, "that is not my axe."

Mercury laid the golden axe on the bank and sprang back into the pool. This time he brought up an axe of silver, but the woodcutter declared again that his axe was just an ordinary one with a wooden handle.

Mercury dived down for the third time, and when he came up again he had the very axe that had been lost.

The poor woodcutter was very glad that his axe had been found and could not thank the kind god enough. Mercury was greatly pleased with the woodcutter's honesty.

"I admire your honesty," he said, "and as a reward you may have all three axes, the gold and the silver as well as your own."

The happy woodcutter returned to his home with his treasures, and soon the story of his good fortune was known to everybody in the village. Now there were several woodcutters in the village who believed that they could easily win the same good fortune. The woodcutters hurried out into the woods, one here, one there, and hiding their axes in the bushes, pretended they had lost them. Then they wept and wailed and called on Mercury to help them.

And indeed, Mercury did appear, first to this one, then to that. To each one he showed an axe of gold, and each one eagerly claimed it to be the one he had lost. But Mercury did not give them the golden axe. Oh no! Instead he gave them each a hard whack over the head with it and sent them home. And when they returned the next day to look for their own axes, they were nowhere to be found.

1   Read this sentence from the passage.

> **He had been working since sunrise and his strokes were not so sure as they had been early that morning.**

The phrase "his strokes were not so sure" shows that the woodcutter was getting –

Ⓐ   angry

Ⓑ   clumsy

Ⓒ   impatient

Ⓓ   uncertain

2   Describe **two** details from the first paragraph that explain why the woodcutter is tired

1: _____

_____

2: _____

_____

3   According to the passage, why is the woodcutter in despair when he loses his axe?

Ⓐ   It is his favorite axe.

Ⓑ   He needs it to earn money.

Ⓒ   He is embarrassed by his mistake.

Ⓓ   He is too worn out to try to rescue it.

4 How is the woodcutter's axe different from the gold and silver one?

Ⓐ   It is simpler.

Ⓑ   It is shinier.

Ⓒ   It is smaller.

Ⓓ   It is sharper.

5 Why does Mercury give the woodcutter all three of the axes?

Ⓐ   He thinks the woodcutter will lose one again.

Ⓑ   He wants to help the woodcutter work faster.

Ⓒ   He is rewarding the woodcutter for telling the truth.

Ⓓ   He believes the axes he fetched may as well be used.

6 Describe **two** details from the first two paragraphs that make the reader feel sorry for the woodcutter.

1: _____

_____

2: _____

_____

7   When Mercury brings up the golden axe, do you think it is surprising that the woodcutter does not claim that it is his? Explain why you feel that way.

_____

_____

_____

_____

_____

8   Read these sentences from the passage.

> **The woodcutters hurried out into the woods, one here, one there, and hiding their axes in the bushes, pretended they had lost them. Then they wept and wailed and called on Mercury to help them.**

Are the woodcutters really upset when they weep and wail? Use details from the passage to explain your answer.

_____

_____

_____

_____

_____

9 In the last paragraph, how does Mercury teach the woodcutters a lesson? Use **two** details from the passage to support your answer.

_____

_____

_____

_____

_____

10 Which phrase best summarizes the main lesson of the passage? Select the **one** best answer.

☐ Beauty is in the eye of the beholder.

☐ A bird in the hand is worth two in the bush.

☐ Honesty is the best policy.

☐ Fortune favors the brave.

☐ All that glitters is not gold.

☐ Don't put all your eggs in one basket.

Practice Set 6

Science Fiction

Space Racing

Instructions

This set has one passage for you to read. The passage is followed by questions

Read each question carefully. For each multiple choice question, fill in the circle for the correct answer. For other types of questions, follow the instructions given. Some of the questions require a written answer. Write your answer on the lines provided.

Space Racing

The green laser beam finished adding my name to the virocraft. "Nayla," it read in dark green letters. Green and dark purple were my favorite colors. I made all the miniature space crafts I built these colors. Finally it was finished. It was about the size of a human boot and looked perfect.

Virocrafts are space drones that can teleport. Teleporting means moving from one place to any other place in an instant. Virocrafts can be transported anywhere on Earth and even beyond. You might find your craft in a thick forest, high in the air, deep under the ocean, or even in orbit around another planet. To fly, you need the coordinates for the flight route, a controller, and goggles that allow you to see where your virocraft is. Building miniature ships was fun. I guess it also helps that my father is a top spacecraft engineer. Racing virocrafts is even more fun.

My father moved my brother and me to this three-ringed planet a few weeks ago. I started going to a new school called Bryton Academy. Bryton always has an annual space derby race. This was the only reason I accepted our new home without complaining. I loved to fly my space crafts any chance I could.

In fact, I could not wait for the race to start today.

"Hi, newbie."

"Eat my space dust, Blaster," I replied.

Blaster was one of the blue Martians in my class and very smart. He had heard that I built space crafts for fun. Every day he would ask about my virocraft, but I didn't tell him much. I thought he was probably trying to steal my secrets. I planned to pass him the first chance possible.

Inside the dome, I looked at the blue holographic board where the racing results were displayed. There were three racing rounds. Then the final race was for the top five surviving racers with the best overall times. The first two rounds were easy for me. The first round was whizzing over sand dunes in a desert and the second was weaving through caves. Then in the third round, I almost lost a wing to a lava rock when we raced on a fire course deep inside a volcano. Thankfully, I still made it into the final top five.

After my virocraft teleported back to my side, I began to examine it. One of the neon green floor lights was out and the purple power panel in the rear was chipped. It was nothing I couldn't fix during the break.

As we waited to start, I eyed my competition for the final. There was Blaster, a green Martian named Tyro, and two other humans. With a deep breath, I entered the race coordinates into my curved steering rod. Then, I adjusted my silver goggles over my eyes. A soft green image of the course route appeared. It was a very short course of only two environments – ocean and space. Our crafts would first teleport to the Balton Ocean and then enter the Spiralax Galaxy.

"Nayla, you barely made it. Show us what you got this time around," Blaster smiled.

I just gave him a smirk and put my hand on my virocraft. Five. Four. Three. Two. One. You could hear the sharp pop as the virocrafts all disappeared at the same time. Through my goggles, I was once again in my ship. This time, I was sailing through the misty green ocean. In the top right corner of my virtual screen, there was a small green box where I could pull up information. I selected "Course Racers" so I could view where everyone else was in the course.

Speeding through the ocean, we were all almost head to head. There was nothing but water and bare ocean floor. I was in third place and Blaster was in second. "You won't be ahead for long," I muttered to myself. The next location for teleporting was coming up. It was risky, but I entered light speed and was the first to shift environments.

Suddenly, the green ocean turned to black space. Almost losing control, I swerved just in time to avoid a gigantic meteoroid. My screen warned of a racer on my tail sporting red and green. It was Blaster. Before I could nudge him into a passing rock, our virocrafts became surrounded by a thick sea of rocky meteoroids.

The finish line coordinates were just in front but impossible to reach. A mass of space rocks formed a tight barrier. There was no way through, and so we would have to go around. Blaster chose to pass me and weave around them from the right side. I chose to go around the left side. I chose wrong. Blaster made a quick dash to the right, found an opening, and made the finish line in seconds. To the left, I remained blocked and had to keep going around. I reached the finish line nearly ten seconds after Blaster.

The loss hurt. It hurt my pride. I was angry. But after years of competing, I had learned something. Both wins and losses happen in races and in life. So when I lose, I just have to shake it off and learn from it. With a heavy sigh, I put my bag over my shoulder to leave. I was defeated for now, but I would be back to compete another day.

"Hey, Nayla."

I looked toward the sound of my name. It was Blaster. He was wearing his medal and smiling. I expected him to gloat or make fun of me.

"Nayla, you were amazing today," he said. "It was only luck that I managed to beat you at the end."

"True," I smiled. "Good luck for you. Bad luck for me. It was a great race, though. Congratulations on the win."

I started to walk away.

"Hey, you're new here right?" Blaster asked.

I nodded.

"You should come join our drone club. We compete in teams all the time. The Planet Games and the Galaxy Games are coming up soon. We could do with some new talent on our team."

"That sounds great!" I said with a big smile. "And maybe we could have a rematch to practice our skills."

Blaster nodded. "I'll take you on any time," he said. "I need someone as good as you to push me. And I'll share with you our technology. You're going to be amazed when you see our lab. Your skills are great, but your machine could be so much better."

"It's a deal," I said. "See you tomorrow."

1   One way you can tell that the passage is science fiction is that it mentions many types of technology. Complete the web below by listing **three** more examples of technology mentioned in the first two paragraphs.

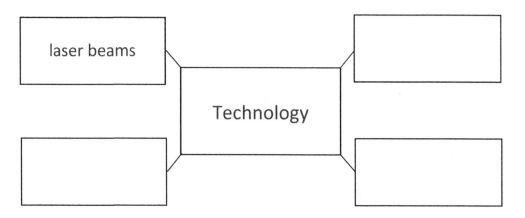

2   What does the art at the beginning of the passage mainly help readers understand?

Ⓐ   why Nayla enjoys making virocrafts

Ⓑ   what a virocraft looks like

Ⓒ   how virocrafts can teleport

Ⓓ   what size most virocrafts are

3   Read this sentence from the passage.

I made all the miniature space crafts I built these colors.

What does the word *miniature* mean?

Ⓐ   expensive

Ⓑ   magical

Ⓒ   powerful

Ⓓ   small

4 Which **two** sentences from the second paragraph best support the idea that virocrafts need to be ready for anything? Select the **two** best answers.

☐ Virocrafts are space drones that can teleport.

☐ Teleporting means moving from one place to any other place in an instant.

☐ Virocrafts can be transported anywhere on Earth and even beyond.

☐ You might find your craft in a thick forest, high in the air, deep under the ocean, or even in orbit around another planet.

☐ To fly, you need the coordinates for the flight route, a controller, and goggles that allow you to see where your virocraft is.

☐ Building miniature ships was fun.

☐ I guess it also helps that my father is a top spacecraft engineer.

☐ Racing virocrafts is even more fun.

5 How does Nayla most likely feel before the race?

Ⓐ angry

Ⓑ defeated

Ⓒ excited

Ⓓ nervous

6   Which sentence from paragraph 7 best shows that Nayla does not trust Blaster?

Ⓐ   *Blaster was one of the blue Martians in my class and very smart.*

Ⓑ   *He had heard that I built space crafts for fun.*

Ⓒ   *Every day he would ask about my virocraft, but I didn't tell him much.*

Ⓓ   *I thought he was probably trying to steal my secrets.*

7   Paragraph 8 describes the first rounds of the race. What is the most important point o the paragraph?

Ⓐ   Nayla flies through a volcano.

Ⓑ   Nayla makes it to the final top five.

Ⓒ   Nayla damages her virocraft.

Ⓓ   Nayla doesn't compete against Blaster.

8   In the passage, Nayla almost loses a wing when she hits a –

Ⓐ   meteorite

Ⓑ   coral reef

Ⓒ   lava rock

Ⓓ   sand dune

9   Read these sentences from the passage.

> **The loss hurt. It hurt my pride. I was angry. But after years of competing, I had learned something. Both wins and losses happen in races and in life. So when I lose, I just have to shake it off and learn from it. With a heavy sigh, I put my bag over my shoulder to leave. I was defeated for now, but I would be back to compete another day.**

A main theme of these sentences is about coping with –

Ⓐ   disappointment

Ⓑ   jealousy

Ⓒ   pain

Ⓓ   sadness

10   Read these words spoken by Blaster.

> **"Nayla, you were amazing today," he said. "It was only luck that I managed to beat you at the end."**

What is Blaster doing in these sentences?

Ⓐ   bragging about his win

Ⓑ   making fun of Nayla

Ⓒ   giving Nayla praise

Ⓓ   trying to trick Nayla

11 Select the **three** situations that are part of the passage that a student reading the passage would be most likely to have experienced. Select the **three** best answers.

☐ moving to a new planet

☐ starting at a new school

☐ trying to win a race

☐ building a fast space craft

☐ meeting people from different planets

☐ joining a school club

12 Complete the diagram below by listing **five** different environments that Nayla flies through in order from first to last.

Environments that Nayla Flies Through

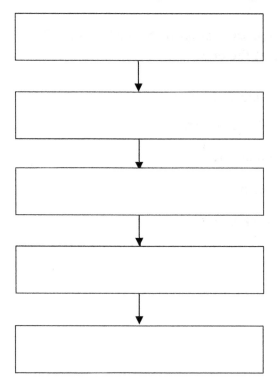

13   How is Blaster lucky to win the race? Use **two** details from the passage to support your answer.

_____

_____

_____

_____

14   At the end of the passage, how does Nayla most likely feel about joining the drone club? Use **two** details from the passage to support your answer.

_____

_____

_____

_____

15 How does Nayla's relationship with Blaster change during the passage? Use **three** detail
from the passage in your answer.

_____

_____

_____

_____

_____

_____

_____

_____

_____

_____

_____

_____

_____

_____

_____

_____

_____

Practice Set 7

Poetry

Set of Two Poems

Instructions

This set has two passages for you to read. Each passage is followed by questions.

Read each question carefully. For each multiple choice question, fill in the circle for the correct answer. For other types of questions, follow the instructions given. Some of the questions require a written answer. Write your answer on the lines provided.

The World's Music
By Gabriel Setoun

The world's a very happy place,
Where every child should dance and sing,
And always have a smiling face,
And never sulk for anything.

I waken when the morning's come,
And feel the air and light alive
With strange sweet music like the hum
Of bees about their busy hive.

The twigs that shake, and boughs that sway;
And tall old trees you could not climb;
And winds that come, but cannot stay,
Are singing gaily all the time.

From dawn to dark the old mill-wheel
Makes music, going round and round;
And dusty-white with flour and meal,
The miller whistles to its sound.

And if you listen to the rain
Where leaves and birds and bees are dumb,
You hear it pattering on the pane
Like a child beating on his drum.

The coals beneath the kettle croon,
And clap their hands and dance in glee;
And even the kettle hums a tune
To tell you when it's time for tea.

The world is such a happy place
That children, whether big or small,
Should always have a smiling face,
And never, never sulk at all.

1   Which phrase from the third stanza describes the sound of the wind?

    Ⓐ   *winds that come*

    Ⓑ   *but cannot stay*

    Ⓒ   *singing gaily*

    Ⓓ   *all the time*

2   Select the line from the fifth stanza that uses a simile. Then explain what the simile helps the reader imagine.

    ☐   And if you listen to the rain

    ☐   Where leaves and birds and bees are dumb,

    ☐   You hear it pattering on the pane

    ☐   Like a child beating on his drum.

_____

_____

_____

3   Which detail included about the miller suggests that he is happy?

    Ⓐ   He works from dawn to dark.

    Ⓑ   He works in an old mill.

    Ⓒ   He is covered in flour and meal.

    Ⓓ   He whistles while he works.

4 Read this line from the poem.

The coals beneath the kettle croon,

What does the word *croon* mean?

Ⓐ glow

Ⓑ sing

Ⓒ wait

Ⓓ yell

5 The poem describes some of the sights and sounds of nature. Complete the table below by listing **two** sights and **two** sounds of nature described in the poem.

Sights	Sounds
1)	1)
2)	2)

6 Compare the first and the last stanzas. Describe **two** ways the stanzas are similar.

1: _____

_____

2: _____

_____

7   Read these lines from the poem.

> **The coals beneath the kettle croon,**
> **And clap their hands and dance in glee;**

The coals are not actually clapping or dancing, but this description helps the reader imagine the coals in the fire. Describe what each phrase helps the reader imagine about the coals.

clap their hands: _____

_____

dance with glee: _____

_____

8   Which statement best describes the poet's main message in the poem?

    Ⓐ   Children should spend every day playing.

    Ⓑ   Children should spend more time outdoors.

    Ⓒ   Children should enjoy every day.

    Ⓓ   Children should enjoy doing helpful work.

9 How does the poem suggest that children should appreciate the little things in life? Use **two** details from the poem to support your answer.

_____

_____

_____

_____

_____

10 How does the photograph relate to the message of the poem? Explain your answer.

_____

_____

_____

_____

_____

The Raven and the Fox

The raven was perched upon a limb,
As a cunning fox looked up at him;
For the raven held in his great big beak
A morsel the fox would go far to seek.

Said the fox, in admiring tones: "My word!
Sir Raven, you are a handsome bird.
Such feathers! If you would only sing,
The birds of these woods would call you king."

The raven, who did not see the joke,
Forgot that his voice was just a croak.
He opened his beak, in his foolish pride –
And down fell the morsel the fox had spied.

"Ha-ha!" said the fox. "And now you see
You have been fooled by flattery.
Vanity, sir is a horrid vice –
I'm sure the lesson is worth the price."

1   Read this line from the poem.

As a cunning fox looked up at him;

What does the word *cunning* mean?

Ⓐ   sad

Ⓑ   silent

Ⓒ   sly

Ⓓ   stubborn

2   Which line from the first stanza tells what the fox wants?

Ⓐ   *The raven was perched upon a limb,*

Ⓑ   *As a cunning fox looked up at him;*

Ⓒ   *For the raven held in his great big beak*

Ⓓ   *A morsel the fox would go far to seek.*

3   Read these words spoken by the fox.

**"… If you would only sing,
The birds of these woods would call you king."**

What does the fox mean when he says that the birds "would call you king"?

Ⓐ   The birds would be scared.

Ⓑ   The birds would be helpful.

Ⓒ   The birds would be jealous.

Ⓓ   The birds would be impressed.

4   Circle the **two** words from the poem that have about the same meaning.

perched	handsome	joke
croak	foolish	pride
vanity	lesson	price

5   What type of poem is "The Raven and the Fox"?

Ⓐ   an ode, a poem written in praise of something

Ⓑ   a narrative poem, a poem that tells a story

Ⓒ   free verse, a poem without a set pattern of rhyme or rhythm

Ⓓ   a lyric poem, a poem in which someone expresses emotions

6   The poem describes the raven's voice as "just a croak." According to the third stanza, why does the raven sing even though his voice is "just a croak"? Use **two** details from the stanza to support your answer.

_____

_____

_____

_____

_____

7   What does the illustration help the reader understand about how the fox feels about the food the raven has? Explain your answer.

_____

_____

_____

_____

_____

8   How does the fox use the raven's pride to trick him? Use **two** details from the poem to support your answer.

_____

_____

_____

_____

_____

9   Select the line from the last stanza that best tells the message of the poem. Then
explain the message in your own words.

☐   "Ha-ha!" said the fox. "And now you see

☐   You have been fooled by flattery.

☐   Vanity, sir is a horrid vice –

☐   I'm sure the lesson is worth the price."

_____

_____

_____

_____

_____

10   Describe the rhyme pattern in each stanza of the poem.

_____

_____

_____

_____

_____

Practice Set 8

Nature Myths

Set of Two Myths

Instructions

This set has two passages for you to read. Each passage is followed by questions

Read each question carefully. For each multiple choice question, fill in the circle for the correct answer. For other types of questions, follow the instructions given. Some of the questions require a written answer. Write your answer on the lines provided.

The Story of the First Pearls

There was once a man named Runoia, and when he walked through the forest, the children would say shyly to one another, "Look, there is the man who always hears music."

It was really true that wherever he went he could hear sweet music. There are some kinds of music that everyone can hear, but Runoia heard sweet sounds where others heard nothing. When the lilies sang their evening song to the stars, he could hear it, and when the mother tree whispered goodnight to the little green leaves, he heard the music of her whisper, though other men heard not a sound.

He was sorry for those other men. He said to himself, "I will make a harp, and then even if they cannot hear all the kinds of music, they will hear the sweet voice of the harp."

This must have been a magic harp, for if anyone touched it, no sound was heard. But when Runoia touched the strings, the trees bent down their branches to listen, the little blossoms put their heads out shyly, and even the wind was hushed. All kinds of beasts and birds came about him as he played, and the sun and the moon stood still in the heavens to hear the wonderful music. All these beautiful things happened whenever Runoia touched the strings.

Sometimes Runoia's music was sad. Then the sun and the moon hid their faces behind the clouds, the wind sang mournfully, and the lilies bent low their snow-white blossoms.

One day Runoia roamed far away till he came to the shores of the great sea. The sun had set, darkness hid the sky and the water, not a star was to be seen. Not a sound was heard but the wailing of the sea. No friend was near. "I have no friends," he said. He laid his hand upon his harp, and the strings gave forth sweet sounds, at first softly and shyly. Then the sounds grew louder, and soon the world was full of music, such as even Runoia had never heard before.

"It is really true," he said to himself. "My harp is giving me music to drive away my sadness." He listened, and the harp played more and more sweetly. "He who has a harp has one true friend. He who loves music is loved by the gods," so the harp sang to him. Tears came into Runoia's eyes, but they were tears of happiness, not of sadness. A gentle voice called, "Runoia, come to the home of the gods."

As darkness fell over the sea, Runoia's friends went to look for him. He was gone, but where he had stood listening happily to the music of the gods, there on the fair white sand was the harp, and all around it lay beautiful pearls, shining softly in the moonlight, for every tear of happiness was now a pearl.

1   What does the illustration at the start of the passage suggest about Runoia?

 Ⓐ He feels sorry for people.

 Ⓑ He is connected to nature.

 Ⓒ He hears music all the time.

 Ⓓ He has few friends.

2   Read this sentence from the passage.

> **He said to himself, "I will make a harp, and then even if they cannot hear all the kinds of music, they will hear the sweet voice of the harp."**

What does this sentence show is Runoia's main motivation for making the harp?

 Ⓐ wanting to entertain people

 Ⓑ wanting people to understand him

 Ⓒ wanting to share the music he loves with others

 Ⓓ wanting the music he hears to be more beautiful

3   The passage refers to how the "wind sang mournfully." What does the word *mournfully* mean?

 Ⓐ angrily

 Ⓑ loudly

 Ⓒ sadly

 Ⓓ strongly

4   Use the details in paragraph 4 to complete the table with a description of how each element of nature responds to the music.

Element of Nature	Action
trees	bend down to listen
blossoms	
wind	
beasts and birds	
sun and moon	

5   In paragraph 6, how does Runoia feel while on the shore of the sea? Select the **one** best answer.

☐   disappointed

☐   embarrassed

☐   frightened

☐   jealous

☐   lonely

☐   nervous

6 Which sentence best supports the idea that the music of the harp comforts Runoia?

Ⓐ *He laid his hand upon his harp, and the strings gave forth sweet sounds, at first softly and shyly.*

Ⓑ *Then the sounds grew louder, and soon the world was full of music, such as even Runoia had never heard before.*

Ⓒ *"My harp is giving me music to drive away my sadness."*

Ⓓ *He listened, and the harp played more and more sweetly.*

7 What is the main purpose of the story overall?

Ⓐ to describe how something came to be created

Ⓑ to tell how someone learned a lesson

Ⓒ to explain the role of something in society

Ⓓ to teach an important value

8 In paragraph 2, the author describes how Runoia "heard sweet sounds where others heard nothing." List the **two** examples of these sounds the author gives.

1: _____

_____

2: _____

_____

9   Describe the personification the author uses in paragraph 4. Use **two** details from the paragraph to support your answer.

_____

_____

_____

_____

_____

10   According to the story, where do the pearls found on the beach come from? Use **two** details from the passage to support your answer.

_____

_____

_____

_____

_____

Why the Cat Always Falls Upon Her Feet

Some magicians are cruel, but others are gentle and good to all the creatures of the earth. One of these good magicians was one day traveling in a great forest. The sun rose high in the heavens, and he lay down at the foot of a tree. Soft, green moss grew all about him. The sun shining through the leaves made flecks of light and shadow upon the earth. He heard the song of the bird and the lazy buzz of the wasp. The wind rustled the leafy boughs above him. All the music of the forest lulled him to slumber, and he closed his eyes.

As the magician lay asleep, a great serpent came softly from the thicket. It lifted high its shining crest and saw the man at the foot of the tree. "I will kill him!" it hissed. "I could have eaten that cat last night if he had not called, 'Watch, little cat, watch!' I will kill him, I will kill him!"

Closer and closer the deadly serpent moved. The magician stirred in his sleep. The serpent drew back, but the magician's eyes stayed shut. It crept closer. It hissed its war-cry. The sleeping magician did not move. The serpent was nearly upon him. However, far up in the high branches of the tree above his head the little cat lay hidden. She had seen the serpent when it came from the thicket.

She watched it as it went closer and closer to the sleeping man, and she heard it hiss its war-cry. The little cat's body quivered with fear, for she was so little and the serpent was so big. "The magician was very good to me," she thought, and she leaped down upon the serpent.

Oh, how angry the serpent was! It hissed, and flames shot from its eyes. It struck wildly at the brave little cat, but now the cat had no fear. Again and again she leaped upon the serpent's head, and at last the creature gave up and slunk away from the sleeping man whom it had wished to kill.

When the magician awoke, the little cat lay on the earth, and not far away was the weary serpent still slowly and gingerly slinking away. The magician knew at once what the cat had done, and he said, "Little cat, what can I do to show you honor for your brave fight? Your eyes are quick to see, and your ears are quick to hear. You can run very swiftly. I know what I can do for you. You shall be known over the earth as the friend of the people, and you shall always have a home in the home of the people. And one thing more, little cat: you leaped from the high tree to attack the deadly serpent, and now as long as you live, you shall leap where you will, and you shall always fall upon your feet."

1   The way the scene is described in the first paragraph mainly makes the setting seem –

Ⓐ   quiet and eerie

Ⓑ   calm and peaceful

Ⓒ   unreal and magical

Ⓓ   hidden and mysterious

2   The first paragraph refers to the "music of the forest." Complete the web by listing **three** sounds the magician hears.

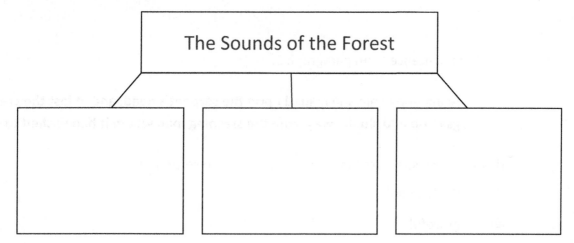

The Sounds of the Forest

3   Read this sentence from paragraph 4.

> **"The magician was very good to me," she thought, and she leaped down upon the serpent.**

What does this sentence show about the cat?

Ⓐ   She wants to make the magician proud of her.

Ⓑ   She feels loyalty to the magician because he saved her.

Ⓒ   She knows that the magician has special powers.

Ⓓ   She believes that the magician will help her again.

4   List **three** actions the serpent takes in paragraph 5 that support the idea that he is angry.

1: _____

2: _____

3: _____

5   Read this sentence from paragraph 5.

> **Again and again she leaped upon the serpent's head, and at last the creature gave up and slunk away from the sleeping man whom it had wished to kill.**

This sentence suggests that the cat defeated the serpent by being –

Ⓐ   determined

Ⓑ   graceful

Ⓒ   quick

Ⓓ   strong

6   What does the last paragraph mainly describe the magician doing?

Ⓐ   warning the cat

Ⓑ   questioning the cat

Ⓒ   rewarding the cat

Ⓓ   punishing the cat

7 In paragraph 2, why is the serpent annoyed with the magician? Use **two** details from the paragraph to support your answer.

_____

_____

_____

_____

_____

8 Describe **two** ways the author creates suspense in paragraph 3.

1: _____

_____

2: _____

_____

9 How does paragraph 4 show that the cat is brave? Use **two** details from the paragraph to support your answer.

_____

_____

_____

_____

_____

10 What action causes the magician to decide that the cat should always land on its feet? Select the **one** best answer.

☐ attacking the snake again and again

☐ hearing the snake's hissing

☐ scratching at the snake's head

☐ leaping down from the tree

☐ hiding quietly in the branches

☐ jumping about to escape the snake

☐ quickly spotting the snake from afar

Practice Set 9

Adventure Story

Was It a Dream?

Instructions

This set has one passage for you to read. The passage is followed by questions.

Read each question carefully. For each multiple choice question, fill in the circle for the correct answer. For other types of questions, follow the instructions given. Some of the questions require a written answer. Write your answer on the lines provided.

Was It a Dream?
By Edith Robarts

Rita grew quite tired of gathering wildflowers while her brother Frank sat by the water busy with his fishing rod.

"He *must* be tired of it by this time! He has been fishing for two hours!" she said, and, swinging her bunch of flowers, she walked to where her brother was sitting.

"*Do* leave off fishing for a while, Frank," she pleaded. "There is a funny-looking animal running about over there in the grass. Come and look!"

Frank laughed.

"I know your funny-looking animals, Rita!" he said.

"Aren't you really tired of sitting quite still?" went on Rita wonderingly.

"I don't think about it," answered her brother. "I want to catch the fish, and to do that I must sit still."

Rita knew she must be contented to wait, so she walked a little way from him and threw herself down upon the bank.

As she lay looking into the water she suddenly felt herself grow very sleepy. A little while after the water began to get so clear that she could see right through it. It grew more and more so until it became just like glass. Rita could see the very bottom of the pond and the fish swimming quickly backwards and forwards.

Then she heard some very funny little voices coming up from the water. This made her look closer, and she soon discovered a small group of fishes. They seemed to be speaking very eagerly together. She saw they were gathered around Frank's line, on the end of which hung tempting piece of bait.

"I tell you, my son," Rita heard the largest fish say to one of the smaller ones, "that is a trap. I have seen hundreds of poor fishes try to swallow that worm, and they have been pulled up out of the water and I have never seen them anymore!"

"But, mother, you must be mistaken!" cried the smaller fish. "If I could just have one little bit. Look what a beauty it is! I am sure there can be nothing to harm me!"

"Inside that worm," continued the big fish, "there is a hook which will catch into your gills, and you will not be able to get away. Then the man at the top will pull you up and up, and you will be pulled out of the water and be gone!"

Still the little fish looked longingly at the bait. Rita wanted to call out and tell him what his mother said was quite true; but somehow her voice refused to come.

The other fishes who were gathered around listening did not say anything, but Rita saw that some of the smaller ones looked at the worm just as longingly as the little one who had spoken.

For a few minutes there was silence in the water. Then, when it thought its mother was looking the other way, the little fish swiftly made a dart forward and tried to swallow the bait. The next moment it was wriggling about and giving faint little cries for help. Its mother swam towards it in great distress.

"Come and help!" she called, in a trembling voice.

All the other fishes surrounded the line. They caught hold of the little fish's tail and held on.

Just as Rita was getting excited, she gave a great start and jumped up from the bank.

"What was that?" she exclaimed aloud.

"I've got a splendid catch. It must be a monster! The line is so heavy I can hardly pull it in!"

It was Frank's voice. Rita suddenly remembered where she was and realized that she must have fallen asleep. She walked slowly to Frank, thinking about her strange dream.

She had only stood by him a minute when—splash!—out flew the line from the water and over went Frank on his back.

It was so funny that Rita could not help laughing heartily—especially as Frank was not at all hurt.

"It's all very well for you to laugh!" he said, when he had got up again. "That was the best catch I've ever had, and the wretched fish must have got off the hook!"

Although Rita felt sorry for Frank, she could not help feeling very pleased that the poor little fish had gotten away!

1   How does Rita feel at the beginning of the passage?

Ⓐ   bored

Ⓑ   enthusiastic

Ⓒ   relaxed

Ⓓ   worried

2   Read this sentence from the passage.

"*Do* leave off fishing for a while, Frank," she pleaded.

Which word means about the same as *pleaded*?

Ⓐ   begged

Ⓑ   demanded

Ⓒ   suggested

Ⓓ   yelled

3   Which phrase from paragraph 8 best shows that Rita is annoyed?

Ⓐ   "must be contented"

Ⓑ   "walked a little way"

Ⓒ   "threw herself down"

Ⓓ   "upon the bank"

4   Which sentence from paragraph 9 is organized by cause and effect?

Ⓐ   *Then she heard some very funny little voices coming up from the water.*

Ⓑ   *This made her look closer, and she soon discovered a small group of fishes.*

Ⓒ   *They seemed to be speaking very eagerly together.*

Ⓓ   *She saw they were gathered around Frank's line, on the end of which hung a tempting piece of bait.*

5   What is the large fish mainly doing when she speaks to the small fish?

Ⓐ   scolding him

Ⓑ   warning him

Ⓒ   encouraging him

Ⓓ   entertaining him

6   In paragraph 10, the bait is described as tempting. Which sentence spoken by the little fish best supports the idea that the bait is tempting?

Ⓐ   *"But, mother, you must be mistaken!"*

Ⓑ   *"If I could just have one little bite!"*

Ⓒ   *"Look what a beauty it is!"*

Ⓓ   *"I am sure there can be nothing to harm me!"*

7   Circle **two** words from the sentences below that show that the fish moved quickly.

For a few minutes there was silence in the water. Then, when it thought its mother was looking the other way, the little fish swiftly made a dart forward and tried to swallow the bait.

8   Describe **two** details from the passage that shows that the mother fish is upset when the little fish gets caught on the fishing hook.

1: _____

_____

2: _____

_____

9   How does Frank feel when he realizes that he has a fish on the line?

Ⓐ   curious

Ⓑ   excited

Ⓒ   guilty

Ⓓ   nervous

10 At the end of the passage, why does Rita laugh at Frank?

    Ⓐ   He loses his fishing rod.

    Ⓑ   He gets pulled into the water.

    Ⓒ   He falls backwards.

    Ⓓ   He catches a very small fish.

11 Read this sentence from the passage.

> **Rita wanted to call out and tell him what his mother said was quite true; but somehow her voice refused to come.**

What does this sentence reveal about how Rita feels about the little fish? Explain.

_____

_____

_____

_____

12 Why do you think the little fish takes the bait even after his mother explains to him what might happen? Explain your answer.

_____

_____

_____

_____

13   When Frank has the fish on the line, he states that it is heavy and feels like a monster. Based on Rita's dream, what is the real reason the little fish feels so heavy? Use **two** details from the passage to support your answer.

_____

_____

_____

_____

14   How does Rita's dream explain why she feels pleased when the fish gets away? Use **two** details from the passage to support your answer.

_____

_____

_____

_____

15 Do you think Rita's experience really happened or do you think it was just a dream? Explain why you feel that way. Use details from the passage to support your answer.

_____

_____

_____

_____

_____

_____

_____

_____

_____

_____

_____

_____

_____

_____

_____

Practice Set 10

Mystery Story

The Mystery of the Missing Salt Shaker

Instructions

This set has one passage for you to read. The passage is followed by questions.

Read each question carefully. For each multiple choice question, fill in the circle for the correct answer. For other types of questions, follow the instructions given. Some of the questions require a written answer. Write your answer on the lines provided.

The Mystery of the Missing Salt Shaker

Tricia was frantic. Her bake sale started in four hours and she still needed to get her cookies in the oven. She was one ingredient away from finishing the dough, and it was nowhere to be found. The recipe called for two pinches of salt. She knew they had just used the salt at dinner last night to season the mashed potatoes, but now that salt shaker had vanished from the kitchen table. She couldn't possibly finish her chocolate chip cookies without this important ingredient.

Tricia's mother was busy working in her home office, and Tricia knew she couldn't disturb her unless it was a true emergency. *But this is a real-life baking crisis*, she thought. Tricia marched up to her mother's office.

When Tricia's mother opened the door, her eyes were wide and worried.

"What's wrong?" she demanded, "Is Leo okay? Is the kitchen on fire?" Tricia blushed.

"Everyone is fine, but I can't find the salt..." Tricia's voice trailed off as she noticed how silly her emergency sounded when she spoke it out loud.

"Sweetheart, the salt is where it always is: the kitchen table. Now, do me a favor and please look before you ask."

Her mother gave Tricia a kiss on the top of her head and closed the door. Tricia sighed. Briefly, she considered asking her younger brother, Leo, but then thought better. Leo was busy outside hopping over each crack in the sidewalk. Recently, Leo had become very superstitious, meaning he trusted in ideas that many thought were foolish. He refused to walk underneath ladders because it was supposed to be bad luck. Most recently, he had heard the superstition, "step on a crack and you break your mother's back." That was why he was carefully walking to his friend's house, being sure to avoid every crack in the sidewalk.

Tricia returned to the kitchen and lifted the tablecloth, just to find a few crumbs left over from this morning's breakfast. She stood on a stool and searched the cabinets, but came out empty handed. Tricia stomped her foot on the floor.

The lawnmower started outside, and Tricia decided to see if her father knew the answer to this mystery. Tricia crossed to the window that looked out over her backyard and prepared to yell to her father. She peeled back the curtains and gasped. A large hole in the window stared back at her. There were pieces of glass on the windowsill and a few pieces of tape attempting to keep the large crack together.

"What in the world?" Tricia yelled out. This caught her father's attention. He glanced up and did a double-take. His expression told Tricia that he had not noticed this issue before.

"Tricia!" her father called back, sounding suspicious and confused at the same time.

"I didn't do it!" Tricia responded with her hands in the air.

She ran out to backyard, turned towards the window and saw something she never expected to see: the salt shaker!

"I'm not sure what happened," Tricia said, "but I have been looking all over for that salt!"

"We'll talk about this when I'm done with the lawn," her father said. Tricia nodded and ran back into the kitchen. Now that she had the salt, she quickly finished off her cookie dough.

As soon as her cookies were in the oven, Tricia went to the window. Her kitchen table sat in front of the window with a chair facing the opposite way. She pulled out this chair and found grains of salt sprinkled on the seat. Curious, she examined the curtains and found more salt clinging to the fabric. The salt shaker was definitely what caused the crack in the window, but who had thrown it? Before she could continue her investigation, Leo walked into the kitchen and froze.

Tricia knew that look on her brother's face. She had found her number one suspect. Her father walked in the door and immediately recognized that expression as well.

"Leo, sit," he instructed gently.

Leo started to turn red as he told the story. Yesterday, Leo had come across a new superstition while he was on the computer. Tricia had found her recipe online and after following a link about salt, Leo discovered that spilling any amount of salt was bad luck. To reverse this luck, you had to throw some salt over your left shoulder. Tricia quickly recalled that Leo had been the last at the dinner table last night. Her mother had served Leo later when he came back from basketball practice.

While his mother left to start a bath, Leo had accidently spilled salt across his dinner plate. Panicking, Leo grabbed the salt shaker and tossed it over his left shoulder.

"I must have thrown it too hard," he managed to squeak out between tears.

"Leo," Tricia started, trying to hold back giggles, "you're only supposed to throw a pinch of salt over your shoulder, not the whole shaker!"

Leo stared back at her and their father looked at his two children. All at once, Leo, Tricia, and their father started laughing. This noise brought their curious mother into the kitchen.

"What is going on here? Did I miss a good joke?" she questioned.

"Nothing to worry about," Tricia replied. "We're just wiping away Leo's salty tears."

The three of them burst out into another round of giggles.

1   The first sentence describes Tricia as *frantic*. Select the **two** words that mean about the same as *frantic*.

☐ baffled   ☐ distressed   ☐ lost

☐ bewildered   ☐ excited   ☐ panicky

☐ determined   ☐ focused   ☐ thrilled

2   Which sentence from the first paragraph shows that Tricia is in a rush to solve the problem?

Ⓐ   *Her bake sale started in four hours and she still needed to get her cookies in the oven.*

Ⓑ   *She was one ingredient away from finishing the dough, and it was nowhere to be found.*

Ⓒ   *The recipe called for two pinches of salt.*

Ⓓ   *She knew they had just used the salt at dinner last night to season the mashed potatoes, but now that salt shaker had vanished from the kitchen table.*

3   Read this sentence from the passage.

When Tricia's mother opened the door, her eyes were wide and worried.

Which literary device is used in this sentence?

Ⓐ   alliteration

Ⓑ   exaggeration

Ⓒ   personification

Ⓓ   symbolism

4   Which detail given about Leo in paragraph 7 is most relevant to the main events of the passage?

Ⓐ   He is Tricia's younger brother.

Ⓑ   He is playing outside.

Ⓒ   He had become superstitious.

Ⓓ   He is going to a friend's house.

5   Read this sentence from paragraph 8.

Tricia stomped her foot on the floor.

This action mainly reveals that Tricia is feeling –

Ⓐ   embarrassed

Ⓑ   enthusiastic

Ⓒ   frustrated

Ⓓ   inspired

6   Read these sentences from the passage.

She pulled out this chair and found grains of salt sprinkled on the seat.
Curious, she examined the curtains and found more salt clinging to the fabric.

What do these sentences represent?

Ⓐ   looking for clues

Ⓑ   finding a suspect

Ⓒ   asking questions

Ⓓ   developing a theory

7   After Tricia finds the salt shaker, what is the mystery she still has to solve?

    Ⓐ   Why does her father think that she did it?

    Ⓑ   How did the salt shaker get in the backyard?

    Ⓒ   Will the cookies be ready on time?

    Ⓓ   Why has nobody fixed the broken window?

8   When Tricia and her father see the look on Leo's face, they both decide that he must have broken the window. What look does Leo most likely have on his face? Select the **one** best answer.

☐	amusement	☐	jealousy
☐	fear	☐	pride
☐	guilt	☐	sadness
☐	hope	☐	satisfaction

9   Read this sentence from the paragraph where Leo describes how he broke the window.

> **Tricia quickly recalled that Leo had been the last at the dinner table last nigh**

What does this detail mainly help the reader understand?

    Ⓐ   why Leo panicked when he first spilled the salt

    Ⓑ   why nobody saw Leo break the window

    Ⓒ   why Leo threw the salt shaker

    Ⓓ   why Leo tried to hide the broken window

10 Describe **two** details from the second paragraph that emphasize what a serious problem Tricia thinks the missing salt is.

1: _____

_____

2: _____

_____

11 The passage mentions superstitions. Many superstitions are actions that are thought to be bad luck. Complete the web below by listing **three** examples from the passage of things that are thought to be bad luck.

Superstitions

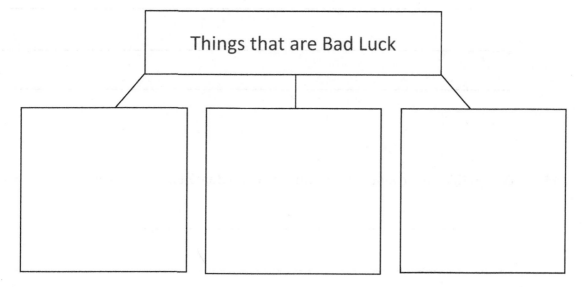

Things that are Bad Luck

12 Describe **two** details from the passage that suggest that Leo feels bad about breaking the window.

1: _____

_____

2: _____

_____

13 Why do you think Leo doesn't admit what he did right away? Explain your answer.

_____

_____

_____

_____

_____

14 Do you think the events are as funny as Tricia does? Explain why you feel that way.

_____

_____

_____

_____

15 Does Tricia find the salt shaker by clever detective work or by accident? Use **three** details from the passage to support your answer.

_____

_____

_____

_____

_____

_____

_____

_____

_____

_____

_____

_____

_____

_____

_____

_____

Practice Set 11

Legend

The Bride of Allan Dale

Instructions

This set has one passage for you to read. The passage is followed by questions.

Read each question carefully. For each multiple choice question, fill in the circle for the correct answer. For other types of questions, follow the instructions given. Some of the questions require a written answer. Write your answer on the lines provided.

The Bride of Allan Dale
A Robin Hood Legend

In the rude days of King Richard and King John there were many great woods in England. The most famous of these was Sherwood Forest, where the king often went to hunt deer. In this forest there lived a band of daring men called outlaws.

They had done something that was against the laws of the land, and had been forced to hide themselves in the woods to save their lives. There they spent their time in roaming about among the trees, in hunting the king's deer, and in robbing rich travelers that came that way.

There were nearly a hundred of these outlaws, and their leader was a bold fellow called Robin Hood. They were dressed in suits of green, and armed with bows and arrows; and sometimes they carried long wooden lances and broad-swords, which they knew how to handle well. Whenever they had taken anything, it was brought and laid at the feet of Robin Hood, whom they called their king. He then divided it fairly among them, giving to each man his just share.

Robin never allowed his men to harm anybody but the rich men who lived in great houses and did no work. He was always kind to the poor, and he often sent help to them; and for that reason the common people looked upon him as their friend.

Long after he was dead, men liked to talk about his deeds. Some praised him, and some disliked his actions. He was, indeed, a rude, lawless fellow; but at that time, people did not think of right and wrong as they do now.

A great many songs were made up about Robin Hood, and these songs were sung in the cottages and huts all over the land for hundreds of years afterward.

Here is a little story that is told in one of those songs:—

Robin Hood was standing one day under a green tree by the roadside. While he was listening to the birds among the leaves, he saw a young man passing by. This young man was dressed in a fine suit of bright red cloth. As he tripped jauntily along the road, he seemed to be as happy as the day.

"I will not trouble him," said Robin Hood, "for I think he is on his way to his wedding."

The next day Robin stood in the same place. He had not been there long when he saw the same young man coming down the road. But he did not seem to be so happy this time. He had left his scarlet coat at home, and at every step he sighed and groaned.

"Ah the sad day! The sad day!" he kept saying to himself.

Then Robin Hood stepped out from under the tree.

"I say, young man!" Robin said. "Have you any money to spare for my merry men and me?"

"I have nothing at all," said the young man, "but five shillings and a ring."

"A gold ring?" asked Robin.

"Yes?" said the young man, "it is a gold ring. Here it is."

"Ah, I see!" said Robin. "It is a wedding ring."

"I have kept it these seven years," said the young man. "I have kept it to give to my bride on our wedding day. We were going to be married yesterday. But her father has promised her to a rich old man whom she never saw. And now my heart is broken."

"What is your name?" asked Robin.

"My name is Allan Dale," said the young man.

"What will you give me, in gold or fee," said Robin, "if I will help you win your bride again in spite of the rich old man to whom she has been promised?"

"I have no money," said Allan, "but I will promise to be your servant."

"How many miles is it to the place where the maiden lives?" asked Robin.

"It is not far," said Allan. "But she is to be married this very day, and the church is five miles away."

Then Robin made haste to dress himself as a harper; and in the afternoon he stood in the door of the church.

"Who are you?" said the bishop, "and what are you doing here?"

"I am a bold harper," said Robin, "the best in the north country."

"I am glad you have come," said the bishop kindly. "There is no music that I like so well as that of the harp. Come in, and play for us."

"I will go in," said Robin Hood; "but I will not give you any music until I see the bride and bridegroom."

Just then an old man came in. He was dressed in rich clothing, but was bent with age, and was feeble and gray. By his side walked a fair young girl. The girl wore a smile, but her eyes were full of tears.

"This is no match," said Robin. "Let the bride choose for herself."

Then he put his horn to his lips, and blew three times. The very next minute, twenty men, all dressed in green, and carrying long bows in their hands, came running across the fields. And as they marched into the church, all in a row, the foremost among them was Allan Dale.

"Now whom do you choose?" said Robin to the maiden.

"I choose Allan Dale," she said, blushing.

"And Allan Dale you shall have," said Robin; "and he that takes you from Allan Dale shall find that he has Robin Hood to deal with."

And so the fair maiden and Allan Dale were married then and there, and the rich old man went home in a great rage.

1   What is the main purpose of the first five paragraphs?

    Ⓐ   to make people curious about the events

    Ⓑ   to help readers appreciate how the world has changed

    Ⓒ   to summarize the story that is to follow

    Ⓓ   to give background information on Robin Hood

2   The illustration at the beginning of the passage mainly represents Robin Hood as –

    Ⓐ   a harper

    Ⓑ   a hunter

    Ⓒ   a leader

    Ⓓ   a traveler

3   Complete the web below by listing **three** details from paragraphs 3 and 4 that the author includes to show that Robin Hood is a good and fair person.

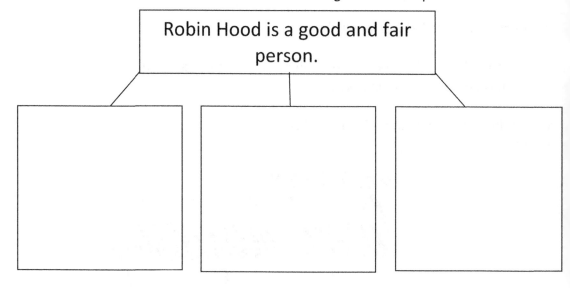

Robin Hood is a good and fair person.

4   Which sentence best helps the reader understand that the story about Robin Hood and Allan Dale is a legend?

Ⓐ   *The most famous of these was Sherwood Forest, where the king often went to hunt deer.*

Ⓑ   *There were nearly a hundred of these outlaws, and their leader was a bold fellow called Robin Hood.*

Ⓒ   *He was, indeed, a rude, lawless fellow; but at that time, people did not think of right and wrong as they do now.*

Ⓓ   *A great many songs were made up about Robin Hood, and these songs were sung in the cottages and huts all over the land for hundreds of years afterward.*

5   Read this sentence from the passage.

As he tripped jauntily along the road, he seemed to be as happy as the day.

Which word could best replace the phrase "tripped jauntily" to show about the same sort of movement?

Ⓐ   roamed

Ⓑ   skipped

Ⓒ   slithered

Ⓓ   trudged

6   What is the first thing Robin Hood asks Allan Dale when he speaks to him?

Ⓐ   where is he going

Ⓑ   why is he looking so upset

Ⓒ   does he have any money

Ⓓ   what is his name

7   Read these sentences spoken by Allan Dale.

> "I have kept it to give to my bride on our wedding day. We were going to be married yesterday. But her father has promised her to a rich old man whom she never saw. And now my heart is broken."

What do these sentences explain?

Ⓐ   why Allan Dale is upset

Ⓑ   why Allan Dale has nothing to give

Ⓒ   why Allan Dale offers to be a servant

Ⓓ   why Allan Dale is walking through the woods

8   The passage describes how Robin "made haste to dress himself as a harper." The phrase "made haste" shows that he dressed –

Ⓐ   carefully

Ⓑ   cleverly

Ⓒ   quickly

Ⓓ   sneakily

9   Select **all** the details below that suggest that the man and the girl are not a good match and should not get married.

☐   The man is dressed in rich clothing.

☐   The man is bent with age.

☐   The man is feeble and gray.

☐   The girl walks beside the man.

☐   The girl is smiling.

☐   The girl's eyes are full of tears.

10   At the start of the story, Robin Hood sees Allan Dale walking through the woods twice. How are Allan Dale's feelings different the second time that Robin Hood sees him? Use **two** details from the passage to support your answer.

_____

_____

_____

_____

_____

11   List **two** details from Robin Hood's conversation with Allan Dale that show that Robin Hood does not help him only out of kindness.

1. _____

_____

2. _____

_____

12   Why does Robin Hood dress as a harper? Explain your answer.

_____

_____

_____

_____

_____

13   The end of the passage describes how the old man goes home angry. If he is angry about not being able to marry the girl, why do you think he did not stand up to Robin Hood? Explain your answer.

_____

_____

_____

_____

_____

14   At the start of the passage, the author describes how some people praised Robin Hood's deeds while other people disliked them. Do you think the story of Allan Dale and his bride is a deed that should be praised or disliked? Explain why you feel that way.

_____

_____

_____

_____

_____

15 Write an essay in which you argue that it was lucky that Allan Dale met Robin Hood. Use **three** details from the passage to support your argument.

_____

_____

_____

_____

_____

_____

_____

_____

_____

_____

_____

_____

_____

_____

_____

_____

Practice Set 12

Personal Narrative

My First Goal

Instructions
This set has one passage for you to read. The passage is followed by questions. Read each question carefully. For each multiple choice question, fill in the circle for the correct answer. For other types of questions, follow the instructions given. Some of the questions require a written answer. Write your answer on the lines provided.

My First Goal
By Marco Morgan

Last fall, I joined the Wilson Soccer Club. I always wanted to play soccer because I have watched my sister play soccer for two years. My sister, Marianna, is six years older than me. She started playing soccer on the girls' soccer team with the Wilson Soccer Club when she was seven. My dad said I had to wait until I was seven too. He said that soccer is a fun sport, but also dangerous. I wanted to play soccer because my sister Marianna is the best goalkeeper on the girls' team. She can stop every goal!

Every Saturday my dad, my mom, and I go to the soccer fields to watch my sister play in a soccer game. My mom brings oranges and juice drinks for her team and I often help her give out the snacks. My sister is my role model. When I told her that I wanted to play soccer too, she said that it is a really fun sport, and both boys and girls love to play soccer.

Finally, when I turned seven years old, my dad said, "Marco, let's go and sign you up for the soccer club." I was so excited to finally get to be on my own soccer team. I joined the boy's 7 to 8 years old team. When I started going to soccer practice I started learning a lot of new things. I thought I knew how to play just from watching my sister and playing in the backyard with my family. I had a lot to learn.

In the beginning, I wanted to be a goalkeeper like my sister. Marianna is so fast, and she can stop everyone from scoring a goal. When I tried to be a goalkeeper, I realized it was very difficult. Marianna is really amazing! Then my coach Mr. Jeff suggested I try the midfielder position. The midfielder position is the best position on the team because you can run a lot, and you can score goals. You're always on the go, so it's very exciting. The midfielder stays in the middle of the field and tries to help both the offense and the defense. I became a very good midfielder quickly. Mr. Jeff said I could be the team's best midfielder if I kept practicing.

At every practice, I ran laps around the field. I wanted to become faster and faster. I wanted to be the best and fastest midfielder on the team. I also learned how to dribble the ball better. Dribbling the ball means that you run with the ball, but you always keep it in your control. You try not to let the ball go too far ahead. I practiced by dribbling the ball through a zigzag course as fast as I could.

My first game was really exciting. My mom, my dad, and my sister came to watch me play. I was so proud to have Marianna watching me play. I was also very nervous. The coach put me in the game after the first 15 minutes of the game had passed. I was very ready to go. I was jumping up and down on the side of the field. When I got to my position, I got scared. I saw the other team coming towards me with the ball and they passed me. I was really upset that they passed me so quickly. Then a little later, I had the ball and another player took it right off me and almost scored. I felt like I was letting everyone down.

At half time, my family came over and told me that it was okay. Marianna said that she was scared when she played her first game too. I felt better and was ready to try again. I really wanted to score a goal for our team. I wanted to show Marianna that I was the best midfielder. In the second half, I gained some confidence. I started running faster, and my teammates passed me the ball a few times. In the last five minutes of the game, the score was 0-1. We hadn't score any goals yet. We needed to score one goal to tie the game. Having a tie score is better than losing. Nobody likes to lose.

I was waiting on the other team's half of the field, when my teammate passed me the ball in front of the net. I knew that I had a chance to score. I dribbled the ball around the other player who was standing in front of me. The other team's goalkeeper was ready. I pretended to kick the ball to the right and waited for the goalkeeper to move. Then I kicked the ball up and to the left. I followed the ball and saw the goalkeeper try to stop it, but the goalkeeper was too far away from the ball. The soccer ball went in the net! I had scored my first goal! My team members were cheering for me and shouting my name. "Marco! Marco! Marco! Marco!"

I couldn't believe that I scored a goal! I really did it! In my first game, I scored a goal! We didn't win the game, but we tied. We tied the game because I scored a goal! I was so proud of myself.

1   According to the passage, why does Marco have to wait until he is seven until he is allowed to play soccer?

Ⓐ   Soccer is expensive.

Ⓑ   Soccer requires strength.

Ⓒ   Soccer can cause stress.

Ⓓ   Soccer can be dangerous.

2   In paragraph 2, Marco says that his sister is his role model. Which sentence from paragraph 1 best supports this statement?

Ⓐ   *My sister, Marianna, is six years older than me.*

Ⓑ   *She started playing soccer on the girls' soccer team with the Wilson Soccer Club when she was seven.*

Ⓒ   *My dad said I had to wait until I was seven too.*

Ⓓ   *I wanted to play soccer because my sister Marianna is the best goalkeeper on the girls' team.*

3   Select **all** the similarities between Marco and Marianna's soccer.

☐   the club they play for

☐   the team they play on

☐   the position they play

☐   the age they start playing

☐   the number of goals they score

4   Which of these would be the best caption for the photograph at the start of the passage?

   Ⓐ   Marianna has been playing since she was seven.

   Ⓑ   Marianna can stop every goal.

   Ⓒ   Marianna is six years older than me.

   Ⓓ   Marianna plays soccer every Saturday.

5   Read this sentence from the passage.

I was so excited to finally get to be on my own soccer team.

Select the **two** words that have the same meaning as "so excited."

☐ amused	☐ nervous	☐ surprised
☐ content	☐ restless	☐ thrilled
☐ delighted	☐ shocked	☐ weary

6   Read these sentences from the passage.

I thought I knew how to play just from watching my sister and playing in the backyard with my family. I had a lot to learn.

What do these sentences suggest?

   Ⓐ   It requires more fitness than he expected.

   Ⓑ   It is more fun than he expected.

   Ⓒ   It is more challenging than he expected.

   Ⓓ   It requires more teamwork than he expected.

7   Complete the web below by listing **three** reasons that Marco gives to explain why he thinks that midfielder is the best position.

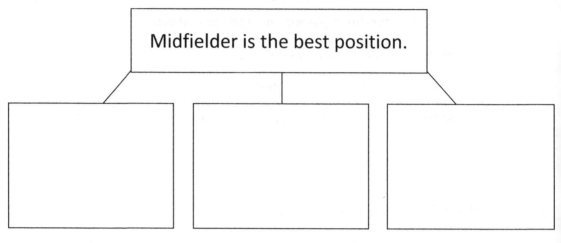

8   Based on the details in paragraph 5, list **two** skills that Marco tries to improve at practice and what he does to improve the skill.

1: _____

_____

2: _____

_____

9   In paragraph 6, Marco describes how he was "jumping up and down on the side of th field." What is the most likely reason Marco is doing this?

Ⓐ   He is excited.

Ⓑ   He is warming up.

Ⓒ   He is cheering his team.

Ⓓ   He is getting his family's attention.

10 Read these sentences from the passage.

> **My team members were cheering for me and shouting my name. "Marco! Marco! Marco! Marco!"**

Why does the author include the dialogue in these sentences?

Ⓐ   to explain why everyone is cheering

Ⓑ   to tell how many goals Marco scored

Ⓒ   to help readers imagine the cheering

Ⓓ   to show how pleased Marco felt

11 How does Marco trying to be a goalkeeper make him appreciate Marianna's skills more? Explain your answer.

_____

_____

_____

_____

12 How is the first half of Marco's first game a letdown? Use **two** details from the passage to support your answer.

_____

_____

_____

_____

_____

13   How does Marco trick the goalkeeper when he scores the goal? Use **two** details from the passage in your answer.

_____

_____

_____

_____

_____

14   Read the last paragraph of the passage below.

> **I couldn't believe that I scored a goal! I really did it! In my first game, I scored a goal! We didn't win the game, but we tied. We tied the game because I scored a goal! I was so proud of myself.**

Why do you think the author uses so many exclamation points? Explain your answer.

_____

_____

_____

_____

_____

15 How do Marco's feelings change during his first soccer game? Use **three** details from the passage in your answer.

_____

_____

_____

_____

_____

_____

_____

_____

_____

_____

_____

_____

_____

_____

_____

_____

_____

Practice Set 13

Play

The Deal

Instructions

This set has one passage for you to read. The passage is followed by questions

Read each question carefully. For each multiple choice question, fill in the circl
for the correct answer. For other types of questions, follow the instructions
given. Some of the questions require a written answer. Write your answer on th
lines provided.

The Deal

ACT I

PLACE: Ali's barber shop
TIME: morning

WOODCUTTER: I have a load of wood which I have just brought in on my donkey. Would you like to buy it, good barber?

ALI: Well, let me see. Is it good wood?

WOODCUTTER: The best in the country.

ALI: I'll give you five shekels for all the wood upon the donkey.

WOODCUTTER: Agreed. I'll put the wood here by your door.

(*The woodcutter lays the wood at the door.*)

WOODCUTTER: Now, good sir, give me the silver.

ALI: Not so fast, my good friend. I must have your wooden pack saddle, too. That was the bargain. I said, "All the wood upon your donkey." Truly, the saddle is wood.

WOODCUTTER: Who ever heard of such a bargain? Surely you cannot mean what you say? You would not treat a poor woodcutter so. It is impossible.

ALI: Give me the saddle, or I'll have you put in prison. And take that—and that—and that!

(*Ali strikes the woodcutter.*)

WOODCUTTER: Ah, me, what shall I do? What shall I do? I know. I'll go to the king himself.

ACT II

PLACE: the King's palace
TIME: an hour later

COURTIER: My lord, a good woodcutter is at the door and begs leave to come into your presence.

KING: Bid him enter. There is none too poor to be received by me.

(*Courtier goes out and returns with the woodcutter, who kneels and kisses the ground. Then he stands with arms folded.*)

KING: Tell me, good man, what brought you here? Has anyone done you a wrong?

WOODCUTTER: Great wrong, my lord. The rich barber Ali did buy a load of wood from me. He offered me five shekels for all the wood on my donkey. When I had put down the load, I asked for my money, but he refused to pay me until I had given him my pack saddle. He said the bargain was "all the wood on the donkey," and that the saddle is wood. He said he would put me in prison if I did not give up the saddle. Then he took it and drove me away with blows.

KING: A strange story, truly. The barber has law on his side, and yet you have right on yours. The law must be obeyed, but—come here and let me whisper something to you.

(*The woodcutter listens smilingly and bowing low, leaves the room.*)

ACT III

PLACE: Ali's barber shop
TIME: a few days later

ALI: Ah! Here comes my stupid friend the woodcutter. I suppose he has come to quarrel about the wood. No, he is smiling.

WOODCUTTER: Good day to you, friend Ali. I have come to ask if you will be so kind as to shave me and a companion from the country.

ALI: Oh, yes, I suppose so.

WOODCUTTER: How much will you charge?

ALI: A shekel for the two.

(*To himself.*) The poor fool cannot pay that sum.

WOODCUTTER: Very good. Shave me first.

(*Ali shaves him.*)

ALI: Now you are shaved. Where is your companion?

WOODCUTTER: He is standing outside. He will come in at once.

(*He goes out and returns leading his donkey.*)

This is my companion. Shave him.

ALI (*in a rage*): Shave him! Shave a donkey, indeed! Is it not enough that I should lower myself by touching you? And then you insult me by asking me to shave your donkey! Away with you!

ACT IV

PLACE: the King's palace
TIME: a half-hour later

KING: Well, my friend, did you do as I told you?

WOODCUTTER: Yes, and Ali refused to shave my donkey.

KING (*to Courtier*): Bid Ali come to me at once and bring his razors with him.

(*Courtier leaves and returns with Ali.*)

KING: Why did you refuse to shave this man's companion? Was not that your agreement?

ALI (*kissing the ground*): It is true that such was the agreement, but who ever made a companion of a donkey before?

KING: True enough, but who ever thought of saying that a pack saddle is a part of a load of wood? No, no, it is the woodcutter's turn now. Shave his donkey instantly.

(*Ali lathers the beast and shaves him in the presence of the whole court, and then slips away amid the laughter of the bystanders.*)

KING: Now, my honest woodcutter, here is a purse of gold for you. Always remember that the king gladly listens to the complaints of his people, and will right their wrongs if he can.

WOODCUTTER: Long live the King!

COURTIERS: Long live the King!

1   Read this line from the play.

> **WOODCUTTER: Who ever heard of such a bargain? Surely you cannot mean what you say? You would not treat a poor woodcutter so. It is impossible.**

Based on this line, how does the woodcutter feel?

Ⓐ   amused

Ⓑ   curious

Ⓒ   shocked

Ⓓ   thrilled

2   At the end of Act I, why does the woodcutter decide to go to the king?

Ⓐ   to complain that Ali has been unfair

Ⓑ   to tell how Ali has hit him

Ⓒ   to show that Ali has not paid him

Ⓓ   to warn the king that Ali is dishonest

3   Read this line from the play.

> **COURTIER: My lord, a good woodcutter is at the door and begs leave to come into your presence.**

Which statement best summarizes what this line means?

Ⓐ   A woodcutter is crying outside.

Ⓑ   A woodcutter needs your help.

Ⓒ   A woodcutter is asking to see you.

Ⓓ   A woodcutter is banging on the door.

4   Select the sentence from the woodcutter's description of the wrong that best shows that Ali has tricked the woodcutter. Select the **one** best answer.

☐   Great wrong, my lord.

☐   The rich barber Ali did buy a load of wood from me.

☐   He offered me five shekels for all the wood on my donkey.

☐   When I had put down the load, I asked for my money, but he refused to pay me until I had given him my pack saddle.

☐   He said the bargain was "all the wood on the donkey," and that the saddle is wood.

☐   He said he would put me in prison if I did not give up the saddle.

☐   Then he took it and drove me away with blows.

5   In the first line of Act III, Ali says that the woodcutter must be coming to "quarrel about the wood." Select the **two** words that mean about the same as *quarrel*.

☐   argue   ☐   confess   ☐   mutter

☐   bargain   ☐   grunt   ☐   whine

☐   bicker   ☐   mumble   ☐   whisper

6   Which sentence spoken by Ali best shows that he does not respect the woodcutter?

Ⓐ   *Shave a donkey, indeed!*

Ⓑ   *Is it not enough that I should lower myself by touching you?*

Ⓒ   *And then you insult me by asking me to shave your donkey!*

Ⓓ   *Away with you!*

7 Read this line from Act IV of the play.

> **ALI (*in a rage*): Shave him! Shave a donkey, indeed! Is it not enough that I should lower myself by touching you? And then you insult me by asking me t(shave your donkey! Away with you!**

What do the words in brackets reveal about Ali?

Ⓐ   how he feels

Ⓑ   where he is

Ⓒ   who he is speaking to

Ⓓ   an action he is taking

8 How does Ali most likely feel when he is shaving the donkey in Act IV?

Ⓐ   confused

Ⓑ   embarrassed

Ⓒ   nervous

Ⓓ   proud

9 What are the woodcutter and the courtiers doing in the last two lines of the play?

Ⓐ   cheering

Ⓑ   complaining

Ⓒ   fighting

Ⓓ   praying

10   The main lesson Ali learns in the play is about being –

    Ⓐ   fair

    Ⓑ   honest

    Ⓒ   loyal

    Ⓓ   smart

11   Complete the table below by listing the place that is the setting of each act of the play.

Act	Setting
I	
II	
III	
IV	

12   At the beginning of the play, Ali asks for five shekels "for all the wood" instead of "for all the firewood." Explain why this detail is important to the events of the play.

_____

_____

_____

_____

_____

13 At the end of Act II, the king whispers something to the woodcutter. What do you think the king whispers? Explain your answer.

_____

_____

_____

_____

_____

14 Read this line from the play.

> **KING: True enough, but who ever thought of saying that a pack saddle is a part of a load of wood? No, no, it is the woodcutter's turn now. Shave his donkey instantly.**

How does this line show that Ali is getting what he deserves? Use **two** details from the play to support your answer.

_____

_____

_____

_____

_____

15   Are the woodcutter's actions a clever way to right the wrong that was done to him by Ali? Use **three** details from the play to support your answer.

_____

_____

_____

_____

_____

_____

_____

_____

_____

_____

_____

_____

_____

_____

_____

_____

Practice Set 14

Poetry

Set of Two Poems

Instructions

This set has two passages for you to read. Each passage is followed by questions

Read each question carefully. For each multiple choice question, fill in the circle for the correct answer. For other types of questions, follow the instructions given. Some of the questions require a written answer. Write your answer on the lines provided.

The Voice of Spring
By Mary Howitt

I am coming, I am coming!
Hark! The honey bee is humming;
See, the lark is soaring high
In the blue and sunny sky,
And the gnats are on the wing
Wheeling round in airy ring.

Listen! New-born lambs are bleating,
And the cawing rooks are meeting
In the elms – a noisy crowd.
All the birds are singing loud,
And the first white butterfly
In the sunshine dances by.

Look around you, look around!
Flowers in all the fields abound,
Every running stream is bright,
All the orchard trees are white,
And each small and waving shoot
Promises sweet autumn fruit.

1   Read this line from the poem.

Hark! The honey bee is humming;

Which literary device is used in the line?

Ⓐ   alliteration, using words with the same consonant sounds

Ⓑ   hyperbole, using exaggeration to make a point

Ⓒ   simile, comparing two items using the words "like" or "as"

Ⓓ   symbolism, using an object to stand for something else

2   Read this line from the poem.

See, the lark is soaring high

What does the word *soaring* mean?

Ⓐ   dancing

Ⓑ   floating

Ⓒ   flying

Ⓓ   singing

3   Which word best describes the tone of the poem?

Ⓐ   chatty

Ⓑ   joyful

Ⓒ   patient

Ⓓ   thoughtful

4   The last two lines of the poem have a message about –

   Ⓐ   seeing the beauty of nature

   Ⓑ   being open to new things

   Ⓒ   looking forward to the future

   Ⓓ   appreciating simple things

5   Complete the web below by listing **three** more examples of animals making sounds.

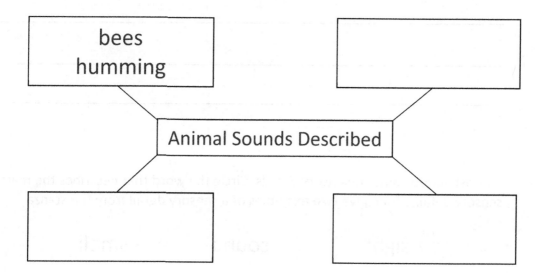

6   List **two** details given in the poem that describe the weather at the time.

   1: _____

   _____

   2: _____

   _____

7 Read these lines from the poem.

And the gnats are on the wing
Wheeling round in airy ring.

A gnat is a small flying insect. Describe the image the poet creates of how the gnats ar moving.

_____

_____

_____

_____

_____

8 The last stanza contains sensory details. Circle the word that describes the main type sensory details. Then give **two** examples of a sensory detail from the stanza.

sight   sound   smell

1: _____

_____

2: _____

_____

9   Which line from the last stanza encourages the reader to take notice of nature? Select the **one** best answer.

☐   Look around you, look around!

☐   Flowers in all the fields abound,

☐   Every running stream is bright,

☐   All the orchard trees are white,

☐   And each small and waving shoot

☐   Promises sweet autumn fruit.

10   Read this line from the poem.

Flowers in all the fields abound,

What does the word *abound* tell about the flowers?

Ⓐ   The flowers are beautiful.

Ⓑ   The flowers are swaying in the breeze.

Ⓒ   The flowers have a fresh scent.

Ⓓ   There are many flowers.

Song of the Sea
By Barry Cornwall

The sea! The sea! The open sea!
The blue, the fresh, the ever free!
Without a mark, without a bound,
It runneth the earth's wide regions round;
It plays with the clouds; it mocks the skies,
Or like a cradled creature lies.

I'm on the sea! I'm on the sea!
I am where I would ever be;
With the blue above and the blue below,
And silence wheresoe'er I go.
If a storm should come and awake the deep
What matter? I shall ride and sleep.

I love, oh, how I love to ride
On the fierce, foaming, bursting tide,
When every mad wave drowns the moon,
Or whistles aloud his tempest[1] tune,
And tells how goeth the world below,
And why the southwest blasts do blow.

I never was on the dull, tame shore,
But I loved the great sea more and more,
And back I flew to seek my rest,
Like a bird that seeketh its mother's nest;
And a mother she was, and is, to me,
For I was born on the open sea!

I've lived, since then, in calm and strife,
Full fifty summers a sailor's life,
With wealth to spend and a power to range,
But never have sought nor sighed for change;
And Death, whenever he comes to me,
Shall come on the wild, unbounded sea.

[1] *Tempest* is another word for a storm.

1   Read these lines from the poem.

> **The sea! The sea! The open sea!**
> **The blue, the fresh, the ever free!**

The rhythm of these lines mainly creates a sense of –

Ⓐ   calm

Ⓑ   fear

Ⓒ   joy

Ⓓ   pride

2   Read these lines from the poem.

> **Without a mark, without a bound,**
> **It runneth the earth's wide regions round;**

These lines mainly show that the sea is –

Ⓐ   active

Ⓑ   overwhelming

Ⓒ   peaceful

Ⓓ   vast

3   Select **all** the phrases from the poem below that are examples of alliteration.

☐   without a bound   ☐   like a bird that seeketh

☐   plays with the clouds   ☐   in calm and strife

☐   like a cradled creature lies   ☐   full fifty summers

☐   southwest blasts do blow   ☐   sought nor sighed for change

4   The third stanza describes how the "southwest blasts do blow." The use of the word *blasts* mainly emphasizes that the winds are –

Ⓐ   common

Ⓑ   loud

Ⓒ   strong

Ⓓ   warm

5   Which statement below best summarizes the speaker's relationship with the sea?

Ⓐ   It is where he feels at home.

Ⓑ   It challenges and tests him.

Ⓒ   It makes him feel lonely.

Ⓓ   It has haunted him all his life.

6   Select the **two** pairs of lines that best support your answer to Question 5.

☐   The sea! The sea! The open sea! / The blue, the fresh, the ever free!

☐   Without a mark, without a bound, / It runneth the earth's wide regions round;

☐   I'm on the sea! I'm on the sea! / I am where I would ever be;

☐   With the blue above and the blue below, / And silence wheresoe'er I go.

☐   If a storm should come and awake the deep / What matter? I shall ride and slee

☐   And a mother she was, and is, to me, / For I was born on the open sea!

7   Does the third stanza describe a calm or a rough sea? Use **two** details from the stanza to support your answer.

_____

_____

_____

_____

_____

8   Read the lines below that contain a simile.

> **And back I flew to seek my rest,**
> **Like a bird that seeketh its mother's nest;**

Why does the speaker compare himself to a bird seeking its nest? What does this simile tell the reader about the speaker? Explain your answer.

_____

_____

_____

_____

_____

9   Read these lines from the poem.

If a storm should come and awake the deep
What matter? I shall ride and sleep.

Based on these lines, does the speaker fear storms? Explain your answer.

_____

_____

_____

_____

_____

10   Describe the rhyme pattern of each stanza.

_____

_____

_____

_____

_____

Practice Set 15

Fairy Tale

Hidden Treasure

Instructions

This set has one passage for you to read. The passage is followed by questions.

Read each question carefully. For each multiple choice question, fill in the circle for the correct answer. For other types of questions, follow the instructions given. Some of the questions require a written answer. Write your answer on the lines provided.

Hidden Treasure
By Jakob and Wilhelm Grimm

Once upon a time there was an old farmer named John Jacobs. He had heard that treasures were found in odd places. He thought and thought about such treasures until he could think of nothing else; and he spent all his time hunting for them. How he wished he could find a pot of gold!

One morning he arose with a bright face and said to his wife, "At last, Mary, I've found the treasure."

"No, I cannot believe it," she said.

"Yes," he answered; "at least it is as good as found. I am only waiting until I have my breakfast. Then I will go out and bring it in."

"Oh, how did you find it?" asked the wife.

"I was told about it in a dream," said he.

"Where is it?"

"Under a tree in our orchard," said John.

"Oh, John, let us hurry and get it."

So they went out together into the orchard.

"Which tree is it under?" asked the wife.

John scratched his head and looked silly.

"I really do not know," he said.

"Oh, you foolish man," said the wife. "Why didn't you take the trouble to notice?"

"I did notice," said he. "I saw the exact tree in my dream, but there are so many trees here that I am confused. There is only one thing to do now. I must begin with the first tree and keep on digging until I come to the one with the treasure under it."

This made the wife lose all hope. There were eighty apple trees and a score of peach trees.

She sighed and said, "I suppose if you must, you must, but be careful not to cut any of the roots."

By this time John was in a very bad mood. He went to work saying, "What difference does it make if I cut all the roots? The whole orchard will not bear one bushel of good apples or peaches. I don't know why, for in father's time it bore wagonloads of choice fruit."

"Well, John," said his wife, "you know father used to give the trees a great deal of attention."

But John grumbled to himself as he went on with his digging. He dug three feet deep around the first tree, but no treasure was there. He went to the next tree, but found nothing; then to the next and the next, until he had dug around every tree in the orchard. He dug and dug, but no pot of gold did he find.

The neighbors thought that John was acting strangely. They told other people, who came to see what he was doing.

They would sit on the fence and make sly jokes about digging for hidden treasure. They called the orchard "Jacobs' folly."

Soon John did not like to be seen in the orchard. He did not like to meet his neighbors. They would laugh and say, "Well, John, how much money did you get from the holes?"

This made John angry. At last he said, "I will sell the place and move away."

"Oh, no," said the wife. "This has always been our home, and I cannot think of leaving it. Go and fill the holes; then the neighbors will stop laughing. Perhaps we shall have a little fruit this year, too. The heaps of earth have stood in wind and frost for months, and that will help the soil."

John did as his wife told him. He filled the holes with earth and smoothed it over as level as before. By and by everybody forgot "Jacobs' folly."

Soon the spring came. April was warm, and the trees burst into bloom.

"Mary," said John one bright spring day, "don't you think the blossoms are finer than usual this year?"

"Yes, they look as they did when your father was alive," said his wife.

By and by, the blooms fell, leaving a million little green apples and peaches. Summer passed and autumn followed. The branches of the old trees could hardly hold up all the fine fruit on them.

Now the neighbors came, not to make fun, but to praise.

"How did you do it?" they asked.

"The trees were old and needed attention," said John. "By turning the soil and letting in the air, I gave them strength to bear fruit. I have found the treasure after all, and I have learned a lesson. Tilling the soil well is the way to get treasure from it."

1   What does the illustration next to the first paragraph represent?

    Ⓐ   what John hopes to find

    Ⓑ   where John should look

    Ⓒ   how the treasure is hard to find

    Ⓓ   why John cannot find any treasure

2   Describe **two** ways the author emphasizes how much John wants to find the treasure in the first paragraph.

1: _____

_____

2: _____

_____

3   Read this sentence from the passage.

> **One morning he arose with a bright face and said to his wife, "At last, Mary, I've found the treasure."**

As it is used in the sentence, what does the word *bright* mean?

    Ⓐ   young and glowing

    Ⓑ   happy and smiling

    Ⓒ   clever and witty

    Ⓓ   bold and shiny

4   Which dialogue spoken by the wife best shows that she is keen to find the treasure? Select the **one** best answer.

☐   "No, I cannot believe it," she said.

☐   "Oh, how did you find it?" asked the wife.

☐   "Where is it?"

☐   "Oh, John, let us hurry and get it."

☐   "Which tree is it under?" asked the wife.

☐   "Oh, you foolish man," said the wife.

☐   "Why didn't you take the trouble to notice?"

5   Which statement best describes how John's wife feels when she learns that he does not know which tree the treasure is under?

Ⓐ   She feels upset because she thinks he is lying.

Ⓑ   She feels annoyed that he did not pay attention.

Ⓒ   She feels sorry for him because he has a lot of work to do.

Ⓓ   She feels confused and thinks he might be tricking her.

6   The wife describes how the trees once bore "wagonloads of choice fruit." This means that they once produced –

Ⓐ   a little poor fruit

Ⓑ   a little good fruit

Ⓒ   a lot of poor fruit

Ⓓ   a lot of good fruit

7 Circle the **two** phrases in the paragraph below that use repetition.

But John grumbled to himself as he went on with his digging. He dug three feet deep around the first tree, but no treasure was there. He went to the next tree, but found nothing; then to the next and the next, until he had dug around every tree in the orchard. He dug and dug, but no pot of gold did he find.

8 Complete the web below by listing **three** ways that people make fun of John.

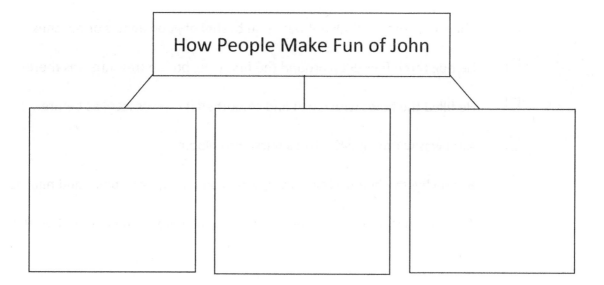

How People Make Fun of John

9   Which sentence spoken by the wife explains how John's actions will help the trees produce good crops?

Ⓐ   *This has always been our home, and I cannot think of leaving it.*

Ⓑ   *Go and fill the holes; then the neighbors will stop laughing.*

Ⓒ   *Perhaps we shall have a little fruit this year, too.*

Ⓓ   *The heaps of earth have stood in wind and frost for months, and that will help the soil.*

10   Which sentence from the passage uses exaggeration? Select the **one** best answer.

☐   I must begin with the first tree and keep on digging until I come to the one with the treasure under it.

☐   There were eighty apple trees and a score of peach trees.

☐   The whole orchard will not bear one bushel of good apples or peaches.

☐   He dug three feet deep around the first tree, but no treasure was there.

☐   He filled the holes with earth and smoothed it over as level as before.

☐   April was warm, and the trees burst into bloom.

☐   By and by, the blooms fell, leaving a million little green apples and peaches.

☐   The branches of the old trees could hardly hold up all the fine fruit on them.

11   At the start of the passage, John says that he knows where the treasure is. Why does John then realize that he doesn't know exactly where the treasure is? Use **two** details from the passage to support your answer.

_____

_____

_____

_____

_____

12   Read this sentence from the passage.

> **"Well, John," said his wife, "you know father used to give the trees a great deal of attention."**

What does this suggest is the real reason that the orchard is not producing much fruit? Explain your answer.

_____

_____

_____

_____

_____

13   What lesson do the events teach John about hard work? Use **two** details from the passage to support your answer.

_____

_____

_____

_____

_____

14   In the last paragraph, John says that he has found the treasure after all. What is the treasure John is referring to? Is it the treasure he expected to find? Use **two** details from the passage to support your answer.

_____

_____

_____

_____

_____

15 Do you think John would have taken care of the trees if he did not have the dream? Explain why you feel that way. Use **three** details from the passage to support your answer.

_____

_____

_____

_____

_____

_____

_____

_____

_____

_____

_____

_____

_____

_____

Practice Set 16

Historical Fiction

Nahum Prince

Instructions

This set has one passage for you to read. The passage is followed by questions.

Read each question carefully. For each multiple choice question, fill in the circle for the correct answer. For other types of questions, follow the instructions given. Some of the questions require a written answer. Write your answer on the lines provided.

Nahum Prince

More than a hundred years ago, our country was at war with England. George Washington was at the head of our army. As you know, he and his men were fighting for our country's freedom.

The English army was larger than our army, and General Washington needed all the men he could get. The regular troops were with him.

In one little town in Vermont, all the strong able-bodied men had gone to the front. News came that the English and the Americans were about to meet in battle. The Americans needed more men and called for volunteers. Old men with white hair and long beards volunteered. Young boys with smooth cheeks and unshaven lips volunteered. There wasn't a boy in the village over thirteen years of age who didn't volunteer.

Even Nahum Prince offered himself. He had been ill as a child and had been left with a terrible limp. He knew he would never be able to walk even a mile at a decent speed. However, he still felt determined to help. He brought out his grandfather's old gun and got in line with the others. He stood as straight and tall as he could – as a soldier should stand.

Soon the captain came along the line to inspect the volunteers. When he saw Nahum, he said, "No, no, Nahum, you cannot go. You know you cannot. Why, you could not walk a mile. Go home, my lad."

Just then the good old minister came by. "Yes, Nahum," he said, "you must stay at home. Who knows if you might even find greater work to do for your country right here?"

And lame Nahum dropped out of the line.

Then the volunteers marched off. Every man and boy in the village left except Nahum Prince. Poor Nahum! His heart was heavy.

"What can I do for my country in this small village?" he said to himself. "Oh, I wish I could be a soldier!"

He walked toward his home slowly and sadly. Just as he passed the blacksmith shop, three horseman galloped up to the door.

"Where is the blacksmith?" demanded one.

"He and all the men and boys have gone to join the army," said Nahum. "There isn't a man or a boy in town except me. I wouldn't be here if I were not lame."

"We cannot have this horse go on without a proper shoe fitted," said the rider to the others. "It slows him greatly, and we shall not reach there in time."

"Why, I can set a shoe," said Nahum.

"Then it is fortunate you are left behind," said the man. "Light up the forge and set the shoe."

Nahum lit the fire, blew the coals with the bellows, and soon put on the shoe.

"You have done a great deed today, my boy," said the rider as he thanked Nahum and rode away.

The next week the men and boys came home and told of a great battle. They told how the Americans were about to lose the fight when Colonel Warner, leading a band of soldiers, rode up just in time to save the day.

Nahum said nothing, but he knew that Colonel Warner would not have arrived in time if he had not set that shoe. And it was really Nahum Prince and Colonel Warner who won the victory of Bennington.

1   The first paragraph of the passage mainly informs readers about the story's –

Ⓐ   narrator

Ⓑ   plot

Ⓒ   setting

Ⓓ   theme

2   According to the passage, why does Washington need volunteers?

Ⓐ   America did not have any trained soldiers at the time.

Ⓑ   The English army was larger than the American one.

Ⓒ   The American army was being quickly defeated.

Ⓓ   America was facing many battles in many different places.

3   Paragraph 3 describes how both young and old people volunteered. Complete the table by listing **two** details the author includes to help readers imagine the old and young volunteers.

How the Author Describes the Volunteers

The Old	The Young
1)	1)
2)	2)

4   Read this sentence from the passage.

He stood as straight and tall as he could – as a soldier should stand.

Nahum most likely stood like this because he wanted to look –

- Ⓐ   young and athletic

- Ⓑ   skilled and experienced

- Ⓒ   honest and sincere

- Ⓓ   strong and capable

5   Select the **two** sentences from paragraph 4 that explain why Nahum would not be a suitable soldier.

- ☐   Even Nahum Prince offered himself.

- ☐   He had been ill as a child and had been left with a terrible limp.

- ☐   He knew he would never be able to walk even a mile at a decent speed.

- ☐   However, he still felt determined to help.

- ☐   He brought out his grandfather's old gun and got in line with the others.

- ☐   He stood as straight and tall as he could – as a soldier should stand.

6   What title does George Washington have in the passage?

- Ⓐ   Captain

- Ⓑ   Colonel

- Ⓒ   General

- Ⓓ   President

7 Read this sentence spoken by the minister.

> **Who knows if you might even find greater work to do for your country right here?**

Which of these is the sentence an example of?

Ⓐ   foreshadowing, hinting at something that will happen later

Ⓑ   flashback, describing an event from an earlier time

Ⓒ   hyperbole, making something sound greater than it is

Ⓓ   symbolism, using something to stand for something else

8 After the volunteers leave, the author states that Nahum's "heart was heavy." What feeling does this phrase describe?

Ⓐ   anger

Ⓑ   disappointment

Ⓒ   jealousy

Ⓓ   tiredness

9 Read these sentences from the passage.

> **"What can I do for my country in this small village?" he said to himself. "Oh, I wish I could be a soldier!"**

What do these sentences mainly suggest about why Nahum wants to volunteer?

Ⓐ   He wants to leave Vermont.

Ⓑ   He wants to have an adventure.

Ⓒ   He wants to help his country.

Ⓓ   He wants to become famous.

10 Read this sentence from the passage.

   "Then it is fortunate you are left behind," said the man.

The word *fortunate* is based on the word *fortune*. Based on this and the word's use in the sentence, what does *fortunate* mean?

 Ⓐ lucky

 Ⓑ rare

 Ⓒ strange

 Ⓓ unfair

11 List **two** details from the last two paragraphs that show how important Nahum's actions were to the battle.

 1: _____

 _____

 2: _____

 _____

12 What do the three photographs at the end of the passage show?

 Ⓐ what Nahum did to set the shoe

 Ⓑ why Nahum decided to set the shoe

 Ⓒ where Nahum learned to set a shoe

 Ⓓ how long it took Nahum to set the shoe

13 Read these sentences from the passage.

> **Soon the captain came along the line to inspect the volunteers. When he saw Nahum, he said, "No, no, Nahum, you cannot go. You know you cannot. Why, you could not walk a mile. Go home, my lad."**

How do you think Nahum would have felt when the captain spoke those words? Use **two** details from the passage to support your answer.

_____

_____

_____

_____

_____

14 Why were the three horsemen so keen to find a blacksmith? Use **two** details from the passage to support your answer.

_____

_____

_____

_____

_____

15 How does the story of Nahum Prince show that everyone can make a difference? Use **three** details from the passage in your answer.

_____

_____

_____

_____

_____

_____

_____

_____

_____

_____

_____

_____

_____

_____

_____

_____

Answer Key

Practice Set 1
The Big Trip

Question	Answer
1	A
2	D
3	A
4	B
5	A
6	The student may list how the vehicles never seemed to slow down, how the cars and people whizzed from place to place, how the people seemed in a hurry, how people knocked into Elena, or how the shopping area was crowded.
7	The student should complete the table with the items below. Elena's mother – perfume Elena's father – green tea Elena's sister – silk dress
8	The student should complete the web with the activities below. snorkeling, played volleyball, built sandcastles
9	green coconuts spicy rice noodles
10	B
11	The student should list how Delhi and Taipei both had markets and how Delhi and Seoul both had fast-paced traffic.
12	C
13	try the local foods
14	The student should give a reasonable explanation of what the phrase "trip of a lifetime" shows about the trip. The answer could refer to how amazing the trip was, how special the experience was for Elena, or how she never expects to be able to do something as great again.
15	The student should give a reasonable explanation of how Elena's time in Thailand is different from her time in the other countries and use relevant supporting details. The answer may refer to how her time is more relaxing, how Thailand is more peaceful, how she spends time in a beach town instead of in a big city, or how she spends time doing fun things at the beach and enjoying nature.

Practice Set 2
The Stonecutter

Question	Answer
1	C
2	A
3	D
4	The student should complete the table with the details below. Paragraph 3 – He feels like his daily work is harder and heavier. Paragraph 5 – He goes home early because he does not feel like doing any more work.
5	B
6	blazed fiercely scorching
7	D
8	The student should complete the web with the three details below. The rivers overflow. The crops of rice flood. Towns and villages are destroyed.
9	C
10	C
11	The student should describe how visiting the rich man's house makes the stonecutter want more or wish for more than he has. The answer should refer to how he wants to be a rich man and have the nice things the rich man has.
12	The student should list how the author states that everything he has is still not enough and how the author describes him looking around for something to wish for.
13	The student should give a reasonable explanation about how you can tell that the events could not really happen. The answer could refer to the use of magic, to the spirit in the passage, to how people cannot really change from one thing to another, or how people cannot become the sun, clouds, or a rock.
14	The student should complete the diagram with the missing items below. rich man → prince → sun → clouds → rock
15	The student should give a reasonable explanation about how the stonecutter learns to be satisfied with what he has. The answer should be supported with relevant details from the passage. The answer may refer to how he changes into many different things, how he is never satisfied no matter what he becomes, how he always longs for more, how he ends up being a stonecutter just like he was at the start, or how the ending describes how he is happy at last because he no longer wishes to be anything but himself or to have anything more than what he has.

Practice Set 3
The Bird with the Broken Wing

Question	Answer
1	The student should match the trees and reasons as shown below. Maple He wants to keeps his leaves neat. Oak The squirrels have taken up all the room. Willow He thinks the birds will break his branches.
2	The student should complete the web with the details below. cold, hungry
3	C
4	I am shivering with cold and weak with hunger.
5	The student may list how the spruce tells the little bird to come to her, holds down her branches so the little bird can jump in, or tells the little bird that she will keep him warm during the night.
6	B
7	The student should complete the table with the details below. Pine protects him from the cold north wind Juniper offers the bird berries to eat
8	A
9	C
10	A
11	D
12	The student should give an opinion on whether the trees were selfish and support the opinion with a reasonable explanation. The student may argue that the trees were selfish because they could easily have helped the little bird, or could argue that the trees had good reasons not to offer shelter.
13	The student should describe how the lines make the reader feel sorry for the bird. The student may refer to how tired the bird is, how the bird has a broken wing, how the bird cannot hold up its wing, how the bird needs to find a place to rest, or how the bird is tired and cold and hungry.
14	The student should explain that both winter and frost are presented as if they are people. The answer should refer to how Jack Frost is a character in the play and how the play refers to King Winter.
15	The student should describe how the spruce, pine, and juniper trees are different from the other trees in Scene I and explain how this affects how they are treated by Jack Frost in Scene II. The answer should describe how they are kind and offer to help the little bird, and how Jack Frost rewards them by allowing them to keep their leaves in winter.

Practice Set 4
Life as a Forty-Niner

Question	Answer
1	B
2	B
3	D
4	B
5	C
6	D
7	B
8	The student may list how the cabin is always damp, how they slept on the floor, how rats and bugs crawled over them, or how they would often get sick.
9	C
10	We worked long hours and recovered very little gold. We made barely enough to pay for our next meal. Still, we could never seem to find enough gold to make any sort of profit.
11	B
12	The student should explain why the brothers did not fight back against the thieves. The answer may refer to how the brothers were outnumbered, how the thieves had weapons, or how the brothers feared for their lives.
13	The student should give a reasonable explanation as to why the brothers mined the new spot secretly. The answer may describe how they did not want any gold they found to be stolen. The student could also infer that they did not want to compete with others or attract others to the area if there was gold there.
14	The student may list how they use their findings to get out of California, how they immediately pack up and leave Coloma, or how they buy a ticket for the next ship leaving San Francisco.
15	The student should describe three reasons the brothers have a difficult time in the gold fields and use relevant supporting details. The student may describe the poor living conditions, the threat and danger of thieves, the hard work it took to find gold, or how they could never find enough gold to get ahead.

Practice Set 5
The Donkey and the Lap Dog

Question	Answer
1	The student should complete the web with the details below. pats, kind words, food or "choice bits from his plate"
2	B
3	B
4	The student should circle any two of the phrases listed below. kicked up his heels, with a loud bray, pranced giddily
5	Now the donkey got it into his silly head that all he had to do to win his master's favor was to act like the dog.
6	The student should complete the diagram with the missing cause and effect below. Effect: The donkey upsets or knocks over the table. OR The donkey knocks the plates off the table. Cause: The donkey jumps up on the master. OR The donkey tries to lick the master's face.
7	B
8	A
9	The student should describe how the donkey's thoughts change in the last paragraph. The student should explain how the donkey no longer wants to be like the dog and wants to work hard like a donkey should.
10	The student should give a reasonable explanation of the humor in the story. The answer could be a general answer describing how it is humorous that a donkey would try to act like a pet dog, or could be more specific and describe details showing the humor such as how the donkey dances around the table, tries to lick the master's face, or how the donkey and the master end up rolling around amongst the broken dishes.

Practice Set 5
Mercury and the Woodcutter

Question	Answer
1	B
2	The student should list how it was late in the day and how the woodcutter had been working since sunrise.
3	B
4	A
5	C
6	The student may list how the woodcutter is poor, how the woodcutter had been working hard all day, how the woodcutter needed the axe, how the woodcutter does not have the money to buy another axe, or how the woodcutter is "wringing his hands and weeping."
7	The student should give an opinion on whether he or she feels that it is surprising that the woodcutter does not claim that the golden axe is his and explain the opinion. The answer could argue it is surprising because he could easily have lied and taken home the valuable axe, or could argue that it is not surprising because the woodcutter seems like a hardworking and honest person.
8	The student should explain that the woodcutters are not really upset and are only pretending to be upset. The answer should show an understanding that the woodcutters have not really lost their axes and are trying to trick Mercury into giving them better axes.
9	The student should describe how Mercury does not give the dishonest woodcutters the golden axe, but whacks them with it and sends them home and then also takes the axes they had hidden.
10	Honesty is the best policy.

Practice Set 6
Space Racing

Question	Answer
1	The student should complete the web with any three of the examples of technology below. virocrafts, space crafts, drones, teleporting
2	B
3	D
4	Virocrafts can be transported anywhere on Earth and even beyond. You might find your craft in a thick forest, high in the air, deep under the ocean, or even in orbit around another planet.
5	C
6	D
7	B
8	C
9	A
10	C
11	starting at a new school trying to win a race joining a school club
12	The student should complete the diagram with the environments listed below. desert → cave → volcano → ocean → space
13	The student should describe how Blaster is lucky to win the race. The answer should refer to how they have to go around a large mass of space rocks, and how Blaster goes right and finds a quick way through while Nayla goes left and takes longer.
14	The student should draw a reasonable conclusion about how Nayla feels about joining the drone club. The answer may refer to her as feeling positive, enthusiastic, excited, or hopeful.
15	The student should describe how Nayla's relationship with Blaster changes and use relevant supporting details. The answer should describe how she does not trust him and is competing with him through most of the passage, but how they start to become friends when she is invited to join the drone club.

Practice Set 7
The World's Music

Question	Answer
1	C
2	Like a child beating on his drum. The student should explain that the simile helps the reader imagine the sound of the rain by comparing it to someone beating on a drum.
3	D
4	B
5	The student should list any two of the sights and sounds below. Sights: twigs shaking, boughs swaying, tall trees Sounds: bees humming, wind blowing, raindrops pattering
6	The student may list how both stanzas describe the world as a happy place, refer to how children should be smiling, and refer to how children should not sulk.
7	The student should list how "clap their hands" helps the reader imagine the sound of the coals or the coals crackling, and how "dance in glee" helps the reader imagine either the movement of the coals or the movement of the flames.
8	C
9	The student should give a reasonable explanation of how the poem suggests that children should enjoy the little things in life. The answer may refer to all the simple things described in the poem, how the poem suggests there is joy to be found everywhere, or how the poem suggests appreciating nature.
10	The student should relate the photograph to the message of the poem. The answer may refer to how the children are smiling and happy, how the children seem to be enjoying being outside, or how the children seem positive and not sulking at all.

Practice Set 7
The Raven and the Fox

Question	Answer
1	C
2	D
3	D
4	pride vanity
5	B
6	The student should give a reasonable explanation as to why the raven sings. The answer may refer to how the raven forgot that his voice was so bad, overlooked the truth because he believed the fox's praise, or was fooled by his own pride.
7	The student should describe what the art shows about the fox's feelings. The answer may refer to how he is staring at the food or how he appears to be longing for the food. The answer should show an understanding that the fox really wants the food but cannot reach it.
8	The student should summarize how the fox uses the raven's pride to trick him. The answer should describe how the fox praises the raven's singing to get him to sing, and how this causes the food to fall.
9	The student should select the line below. Vanity, sir is a horrid vice – The student should summarize the message in his or her own words. The answer should refer to how being too proud or too vain can lead to problems or how being vain is a bad trait to have.
10	The student should describe how there are two pairs of rhyming lines or how the first two lines rhyme and the last two lines rhyme.

Practice Set 8
The Story of the First Pearls

Question	Answer
1	B
2	C
3	C
4	The student should complete the table with the missing details below. blossoms – poke their heads out wind – hushes beasts and birds – gather around him sun and moon – stand still
5	lonely
6	C
7	A
8	The student should list the lilies singing their evening song to the stars and the mother tree whispering goodnight to the leaves.
9	The student should give a reasonable description of the personification in paragraph 4. The answer could describe generally how elements of nature are described as if they have human thoughts, feelings, or motivations. The answer could refer to specific examples like the trees bending their branches to listen, the blossoms putting their heads out shyly, or the sun and the moon standing still in the heavens.
10	The student should explain that each of Runoia's tears of joy become a pearl. The answer should refer to how Runoia cries with happiness as he feels accepted and loved by the gods, and how those tears are left behind as pearls.

Practice Set 8
Why the Cat Always Falls Upon Her Feet

Question	Answer
1	B
2	The student should complete the web with the three sounds below. the birds singing, the wasp buzzing, the leaves rustling
3	B
4	The student should list how the serpent hissed, how flames shot from its eyes, and how it struck wildly at the cat.
5	A
6	C
7	The student should describe how the serpent was going to eat the cat but the magician warned the cat. The answer may refer to how the serpent says "I could have eaten that cat last night" and how the serpent describes the magician saying "watch, little cat, watch."
8	The student may list how the author describes the serpent slowly moving toward the magician, how the author keeps referring to how the magician is still sleeping, how the author makes the reader hope that the magician will wake up, or how the author uses specific phrases like "closer and closer" and "nearly upon him."
9	The student should describe how the cat feels afraid and knows that she is much smaller than the snake, but is brave enough to attack the snake anyway.
10	leaping down from the tree

Practice Set 9
Was It a Dream?

Question	Answer
1	A
2	A
3	C
4	B
5	B
6	C
7	swiftly dart
8	The student may list how the mother swims toward the fish, is in great distress, calls for the other fish to help, or speaks in a trembling voice.
9	B
10	C
11	The student should describe how the sentence shows that Rita cares for the little fish or is worried about the little fish. The answer should refer to how she wants to warn the little fish and stop him from getting hurt.
12	The student should give a reasonable explanation as to why the little fish takes the bait. The student may infer that the little fish does not really believe there is any danger or finds the bait too tempting and cannot stop himself from trying it.
13	The student should explain that the line feels heavy because all the other fish grab hold of the little fish's tail and pull.
14	The student should relate Rita's dream to how she feels pleased when the fish gets away. The answer could refer to how the dream makes Rita see the situation from the fish's point of view, makes Rita care about the fish, or makes Rita feel sorry for the fish.
15	The student should argue that what happened was just a dream. The student should include a reasonable explanation of why he or she feels that way and use relevant supporting details. The answer should describe how Rita's experiences are not things that could really happen and refer to how Rita sees fish having conversations with each other.

Practice Set 10
The Mystery of the Missing Salt Shaker

Question	Answer
1	distressed panicky
2	A
3	A
4	C
5	C
6	A
7	B
8	guilt
9	B
10	The student may list how Tricia knows she should not disturb her mother unless it is an emergency, thinks of the problem as a "real-life baking crisis," or marches to her mother's office.
11	The student should complete the web with the three actions or events that are bad luck listed below. stepping on a crack, walking under a ladder, spilling salt
12	The student may list how Leo turns red as he tells the story, says he must have thrown it too hard, has a squeaky voice, or is in tears.
13	The student should make a reasonable inference about why Leo didn't admit what he did right away and explain the inference. The answer could infer that he was embarrassed, upset, or worried that he would be in trouble.
14	The student should give an opinion on whether he or she thinks that the events are funny and explain the opinion. The student could argue that it is funny because he should have thrown a little salt instead of the whole shaker, or could argue that it was not funny because he did serious damage.
15	The student should explain that Tricia finds the salt shaker by accident. The answer should refer to how she only sees the broken window because she is about to yell out to her father, and only finds the salt shaker when she runs out to the backyard after seeing the broken window.

Practice Set 11
The Bride of Allan Dale

Question	Answer
1	D
2	B
3	The student may list how Robin Hood divided any items taken fairly, only harmed rich men who did no work, was always kind to the poor, or often sent help to the poor.
4	D
5	B
6	C
7	A
8	C
9	The man is bent with age. The man is feeble and gray. The girl's eyes are full of tears.
10	The student should describe how Allan Dale is upset the second time instead of very happy. The answer may describe how Allan Dale is sighing, groaning, and referring to "the sad day."
11	The student should list how Robin Hood asks for gold or a fee if he helps and how Allan promises to be Robin's servant in exchange for help.
12	The student should explain that Robin Hood dresses as a harper so that he can get into the church where the wedding is to take place.
13	The student should give a reasonable explanation as to why the old man did not stand up to Robin Hood. The answer could infer that the man was too old to take on Robin Hood or that the man was afraid of Robin Hood and his team of twenty men armed with long bows.
14	The student should give an opinion on whether he or she feels that the deed should be praised or disliked. Either answer is acceptable as long as it is supported with a reasonable explanation. For example, the student may say it should be praised because he helped two young people get married or because he stood up for a poor young girl, or could say that it should be disliked because he used force and fear to get his way.
15	The student should write an essay arguing that it was lucky that Allan Dale met Robin Hood and use relevant supporting details in the argument. The essay could refer to how unhappy Allan Dale was, how much Allan Dale wanted to marry the girl, how wrong it was that the girl was made to marry an old man, or how Robin Hood helped Allan Dale and his new wife find happiness.

Practice Set 12
My First Goal

Question	Answer
1	D
2	D
3	the club they play for the age they start playing
4	B
5	delighted thrilled
6	C
7	The student should complete the web with any three of the details below. You run a lot. / You can score goals. / You are always on the go. / It is exciting.
8	The student should list how Marco runs laps around the field to become faster and how he dribbles the ball through a zigzag course to improve his dribbling.
9	A
10	C
11	The student should describe how Marco finds goalkeeping very difficult and how this makes him appreciate how skilled his sister is even more.
12	The student should describe how the first half is a letdown for Marco. The answer may refer to how the other team pass him, how someone takes the ball from him and almost scores, or how he feels like he is letting his team down.
13	The student should describe how Marco tricks the goalkeeper by pretending to kick the ball to the right, but then actually kicking the ball to the left.
14	The student should give a reasonable explanation of why the author uses exclamation points. The answer may refer to how he wants to show his excitement or wants the reader to understand how great he feels about scoring the goal.
15	The student should give a reasonable summary of how Marco's feelings change during his first game and use relevant supporting details. The answer should refer to how he feels upset or disappointed in the first half, feels more determined and more confident in the second half, and then feels great when he scores a goal.

Practice Set 13
The Deal

Question	Answer
1	C
2	A
3	C
4	He said the bargain was "all the wood on the donkey," and that the saddle is wood.
5	argue bicker
6	B
7	A
8	B
9	A
10	A
11	The student should complete the table with the places below. I – Ali's barber shop II – the King's palace III – Ali's barber shop IV – the King's palace
12	The student should explain how asking for all the wood instead of all the firewood means that he has tricked the woodcutter into giving him the wood saddle. The answer may refer to how this is how Ali unfairly tricks the woodcutter, which then leads to the woodcutter asking the king for help and finding a way to get even.
13	The student should explain that the king must be whispering the plan to the woodcutter to tell him how to get even with Ali. The answer may refer to how the king is telling the woodcutter how to trick Ali into having to shave his donkey.
14	The student should give a reasonable explanation of how the line shows that Ali is getting what he deserves. The answer should refer to Ali's previous actions in tricking the woodcutter into having to give up the saddle.
15	The student should give an opinion on whether the woodcutter's actions are a clever way to right the wrong that was done to him. The student may argue either way as long as the opinion is supported with a reasonable explanation.

Practice Set 14
The Voice of Spring

Question	Answer
1	A
2	C
3	B
4	C
5	The student should complete the web with the examples below. lambs bleating, cawing rooks, birds singing
6	The student should list the reference to the "blue and sunny sky" and the reference to the butterfly dancing by "in the sunshine."
7	The student should give a reasonable description of the image of the gnats. The answer should refer to them as flying around in circles and may infer that they are peaceful, beautiful, or joyful. The answer may refer to how they are "on the wing," "wheeling round," or in "airy ring."
8	The student should circle the word "sight." The student may list the flowers in the fields, the bright running streams, the white orchard trees, or the small waving plant shoots.
9	Look around you, look around!
10	D

Practice Set 14
Song of the Sea

Question	Answer
1	C
2	D
3	like a cradled creature lies southwest blasts do blow full fifty summers sought nor sighed for change
4	C
5	A
6	I'm on the sea! I'm on the sea! / I am where I would ever be; And a mother she was, and is, to me, / For I was born on the open sea!
7	The student should explain that the third stanza describes a rough sea. The student should use details from the stanza to support the answer. The answer may refer to words and phrases used to describe the sea such as "fierce," "foaming," or "bursting tide." The answer may also refer to specific details or images such as the mad waves drowning the moon, the whistling of the storm, or the strong winds.
8	The student should give a reasonable interpretation of the simile and explain why the speaker compares himself to a bird seeking its nest. The answer may refer to how the speaker feels at home on the sea, feels safe and comforted by the sea, or always feels like returning to the sea he knows so well.
9	The student should identify that the speaker does not fear storms. The answer should refer to how he suggests it does not matter if there is a storm and describes just riding out the storm and sleeping through it.
10	The student should explain that there are three pairs of rhyming lines. The answer may state that the first two lines rhyme, the middle two lines rhyme, and the last two lines rhyme.

Practice Set 15
Hidden Treasure

Question	Answer
1	A
2	The student should list how John could think about nothing but treasure and how John spent all his time hunting for treasure.
3	B
4	"Oh, John, let us hurry and get it."
5	B
6	D
7	The student should circle the phrases "the next and the next" and "dug and dug."
8	The student should complete the web by listing the three details below. make jokes about digging for treasure, call the orchard "Jacobs' folly," ask John how much money he got from the holes
9	D
10	By and by, the blooms fell, leaving a million little green apples and peaches.
11	The student should explain that John saw the treasure under a tree in his dream, but then doesn't know which tree to look under because there was only one tree in the dream.
12	The student should explain that this sentence suggests that the trees are not producing much fruit because they are not being looked after well like they once were.
13	The student should describe how John learns about the importance of hard work, how hard work pays off, or how hard work is needed to achieve something. The answer may refer to how John's hard work in digging the holes is rewarded with good crops, or how John tells how the attention he gave the trees made them bear a lot of fruit.
14	The student should explain that John is referring to the fruit the trees produced as the treasure. The answer should show an understanding that John is not referring to a pot of gold like he once imagined finding.
15	The student should give an opinion on whether John would have taken care of the trees if he did not have the dream. The opinion should be supported with relevant supporting details. The answer may refer to how he was not taking good care of the trees before the dream, how his dream of finding treasure tricked him into taking better care of the trees, or how he only dug holes around the trees because he was searching for the treasure he saw in his dream.

Practice Set 16
Nahum Prince

Question	Answer
1	C
2	B
3	The student should complete the table with the details below. The Old – white hair, long beards The Young – smooth cheeks, unshaven lips
4	D
5	He had been ill as a child and had been left with a terrible limp. He knew he would never be able to walk even a mile at a decent speed.
6	C
7	A
8	B
9	C
10	A
11	The student may list how the Americans were about to lose the fight, how Colonel Warner saved the day, how Colonel Warner would not have been there in time if the shoe had not been set, or how it was really Nahum Prince and Colonel Warner that won the battle.
12	A
13	The student should give a reasonable description of how Nahum would have felt. Nahum could be described as being disappointed, sad, angry, or embarrassed. The student may describe how he really wanted to volunteer or how he felt upset that he was unable to help.
14	The student should explain that the horsemen were rushing to reach the battle, but would not reach it in time because they had a horse that needed a proper shoe fitted.
15	The student should give a reasonable explanation of how the story of Nahum Prince shows that everyone can make a difference and use relevant supporting details. The answer may refer to how Nahum Prince could not play a role as a soldier, but played an important role when he set the shoe. The answer may describe how Nahum Prince wasn't expected to be important because he was lame, but ended up helping the Americans win the battle.

Made in the USA
Middletown, DE
29 August 2024

59955008R00104